CW01082226

Did the Spirit of God Say That?

27 Ways to Judge Prophecy

Jennifer LeClaire

Author of *The Heart of the Prophetic*

Did the Spirit of God Say That? 27 Ways to Judge Prophecy

Copyright © Jennifer LeClaire 2011

Published by Jennifer LeClaire Ministries

P.O. Box 3953

Hallandale Beach, Fla. 33008

305-467-4284

www.jenniferleclaire.org

DEDICATION

This book is dedicated to all those believers who hunger for the authentic voice of God, to any who have been hurt by prophetic ministry, and to every prophet who labors diligently to equip the saints to discern the voice of the Lord for themselves.

TABLE OF CONTENTS

PREFACE

Just like you, I love the voice of God. There is nothing more thrilling than to hear the voice of the Master offering edification, exhortation and comfort, either directly into your born-again spirit or through the mouth of an anointed vessel of God.

True prophetic ministry is vital in this hour. But let's face it. Not all "prophetic" utterances come from God. Prophetic words come from one of three places: the Spirit of God, the human spirit or an evil spirit. Therefore, we have to judge prophetic words—all prophetic words—regardless of whether we hear them in our own spirits or through the prophetic ministry of another.

I've seen far too much misunderstanding of prophetic ministry, heard far too many prophetic utterances that spoke to the idolatry in a person's heart, and witnessed far too many erroneous prophecies that originated out of man's will to generate a profit. Don't get me wrong. I've also heard plenty of true, bona fide prophetic words—and I've seen them come to pass. That's why the Word of God admonishes us to:

"Despise not prophesyings. Prove all things; hold fast that which is good" (1 Thessalonians 5:20-21).

I wrote this book to equip you to prove all things; to better discern the voice of God for yourself so you can have confidence in His leading and reject anything that would derail you. I wrote this book to help you confidently answer one question in the face of prophetic utterances: Did the Spirit of God say that?

We need to learn to hold fast to that which is good; to do war with the prophetic word; to do our part to cooperate with God to ensure conditional prophetic words come to pass. But we also need to let go of those words that aren't "good." We need to be careful not to receive prophetic directives over our lives that did not originate from the Spirit of God. Such words could not only lead us straight out of the will of God— such words could lead us into destruction. That's the enemy's plan, and if he can use a well-meaning prophet or a false prophet (or anyone else) to utter a convincing error over your life, he'll do it every chance he gets.

Yes, the prophet has a responsibility to ensure he is flowing with the Spirit of God. The spirit of the prophet is subject to the prophet (1 Corinthians 14:32). But we can't put all the responsibility on the prophet. Even the most God-fearing, genuine prophets make mistakes now and again. No one is perfect except Jesus. So we must judge prophecy. We must take the responsibility upon ourselves to try the spirits, to prove all things. It's up to us to either receive the prophetic word in truth, put it on the shelf and forget about it, or reject and sometimes bind up words that are false.

My prayer is that this book will give you new perspectives on judging prophetic words. Ultimately, the only test we need is the Bible test. Does it line up with the written Word of God? The Word and the Spirit agree. But because I realize from practical prophetic ministry that it's not always easy or even possible to match a prophetic utterance with a specific Scripture—or even the spirit of the Scripture's intention—I wanted to introduce some additional angles, some different ways to think about the prophetic word. After you read this book, I believe you'll walk away with greater discernment and a better understanding of what true prophetic ministry is all about.

PART ONE

THE BIBLE-BASED TESTS

All scripture is given by inspiration of God, and is profitable for doctrine, for reproof, for correction, for instruction in righteousness: That the man of God may be perfect, thoroughly furnished unto all good works.

— 2 Timothy 3:16-17

First and foremost, we should look to the Bible when judging a prophetic word. All Scripture is God-breathed and is useful for teaching, rebuking, correcting and training in righteousness.

All true prophecy is also God-breathed. If Scripture is inspired by God, and if true prophetic utterances are inspired by God, then the written Word should agree with the spirit of the prophetic word.

The Word of God is the ultimate benchmark against which we should measure a prophetic word from anybody who utters "thus saith the Lord" (or any modern variation of the phrase). Our first six means of judging prophecy, therefore, are based on the Word of God.

CHAPTER 1
TRY THE SPIRITS

Beloved, believe not every spirit, but try the spirits whether they are of God: because many false prophets are gone out into the world.

— 1 John 4:1

Every Holy Ghost-filled believer can prophesy—and many do. With so many "prophetic words" floating around it becomes vital to learn how to judge these utterances.

Whether a veteran prophet prophesies what says the Spirit of God over our life in a prayer line, or Sister Christian offers us a word from the Lord in the parking lot, or we simply receive a rhema word from God for yourself, we must try the spirits.

We must ask, "Did the Spirit of God say that?" It's not a suggestion; it's a directive in the Word of God for our protection.

Beloved, believe not every spirit, but try the spirits whether they are of God: because many false prophets are gone out into the world.

1 John 4:1

There is only one spirit that is infallible—and that's the Spirit of God. Prophecy comes from one of three sources: the Holy Spirit, the human spirit or an evil spirit. Our spirit bears witness to the Holy Spirit, but we cannot offer true prophetic words out of our own spirits.

Our spirits may be full of the Word and we can certainly draw from our spirits to encourage someone with the Word. But we should only prophesy "thus saith the Lord" when there is an unction, a bubbling forth of the Holy Spirit, to speak. If we prophesy without that unction, we are in danger of tapping into our own spirit, or worse, an evil spirit.

Don't Put Your Faith On a False Spirit

The Apostle John, inspired by the Holy Spirit, warned believers not to believe every spirit. The Amplified Bible translates 1 John 4:1 this way: "Do not put faith in every spirit, but prove (test) the spirits to discover whether they proceed from God." And The Message Bible really drives home the point in plain language: "My dear friends, don't believe everything you hear. Carefully weigh and examine what people tell you. Not everyone who talks about God comes from God."

Once, when I was meditating on 1 John 4:1 the second half of the Verse seemed to leap off the page. Specifically, the word "because" struck my spirit. Don't believe every spirit, John writes, but test the spirits to see whether they are of God because ... Because why? If a pastor or a prophet or some other Christian is prophesying in the name of the Lord, why is it necessary to test the spirits in the first place? Shouldn't a minister of the Gospel be telling the truth? Indeed, a minister of the Gospel should. But John says we have to try the spirits because ... because many false prophets have gone out into the world.

Don't get me wrong. Just because someone misses it doesn't make him a false prophet. In my experience, it's the motive of the heart that classifies a person as such. Of course, the existence of false prophets isn't the only reason the Bible exhorts us to judge a prophetic word. But it is one that John emphasized.

And it leads me to a key point: When judging prophecy, we need to focus on the spirit behind the words rather than the words themselves only. Many times, when we hear a prophetic word, it sounds completely accurate on the surface. But just because the word is accurate doesn't mean it's from God. Familiar spirits could be in operation.

Remember the woman who was following the Apostle Paul and his team for many days, shouting, "These men are servants of the Most High God, who are telling you the way to be saved"? The Bible says she kept this up for many days. Finally, Paul became so troubled that he turned around and said to the spirit, "In the name of Jesus Christ I command you to come out of her!" What this woman was saying was true. Paul and his team were servants of God preaching the true way of salvation. But the spirit behind the words was not of God. Paul took some time to discern the source, and when he settled in his spirit that it was not coming from God he took authority over that spirit (Acts 16:17-18). If Paul had embraced this prophetic utterance as true, the spirit in that woman could have gained credibility the devil could have later used to deceive people on his team. I'm not saying we should confront every person who delivers a prophecy out of the wrong spirit. That's not always wise. But we should discern the source of the utterance and reject what does not come from God.

Building Prophetic Muscles

Here's the deal: We want to encourage the army of believers to share what they feel God is saying to them. First, because we want to know what God is saying and He will speak through different people at different times. (Don't negate a potential prophetic word until you judge it—no matter who it comes from. Remember, God once used a donkey.) Second, we want to judge the word so we can equip believers. We can use poor prophecy from a sincere believer as a learning experience. Notice I say "poor prophecy." Poor prophecy is not accurate, but it doesn't set out to deceive as does false prophecy. Big difference. But you still can't put your faith on either.

Prophetic exercises help to sharpen the believer's ears to the voice of God—and other spirits—so they can discern between the righteous and the wicked. Jesus said, "My sheep hear my voice, and I know them, and they follow Me" (John 10:27). Now, when we read this Scripture we usually stop at "My sheep hear my voice." But the latter phrase of that verse is vital: "and they follow Me." I believe the Holy Spirit is earnestly trying to get through to us—and that we oft hear Him but we don't always follow that unction. That's where we get into trouble, or at least get inconvenienced.

Unfortunately, I have too many examples of this to share from my own life. Thankfully, the consequences of dismissing that inward witness during my training process were relatively benign. For example, one day I was in a wholesale club where you can purchase goods at deep discounts. In the checkout line they have a debit card payment system that allows you to get back some cash, $10, $20, $40, $60 or $100, from your bank account.

While I was wrapping up the transaction, I felt an unction to get some cash. But my mind began to reason with the inner witness, arguing that I was headed home and didn't need to withdrawal cash that I might frivolously spend. (If you don't have a plan for your cash, it takes on a mind of its own and wastes itself.) In a matter of seconds, my natural mind overcame the supernatural unction.

Then it happened. A friend called and asked if I wanted to hook up to play some putt-putt golf. I always loved putt-putt golf and since it was a beautiful day outside, I accepted the invitation. The only problem was, when I got to the putt-putt park the man in the little beach shack only accepted cash. No credit cards allowed. No debit cards accepted. No cash, no putt-putt. I spent a good 15 to 20 minutes running up and down the beach looking for an ATM machine so I could withdrawal the cash. It was a little frustrating, mostly because I quickly realized that the Holy Spirit knew I would need the cash—and I didn't listen.

Failing to Heed the Voice of the Lord

Another time the consequences were more devastating. This example illustrates the danger of allowing a person to influence you when you know you've heard from God. This can happen especially when you wish it wasn't God you heard. The Holy Ghost told me that there was a season of separation coming with a close friend. Who wants to believe that? Exactly. It troubled me, so I told my friend what the Holy Ghost said. Well, that was the wrong thing to do. I should have kept my mouth shut and prayed.

My friend didn't receive the word. In fact, not only did she not receive the word, she told me I was listening to the devil. By this time I knew the difference between the voice of the Lord and the voice of the enemy. I was confident I was hearing from the Lord, but my friend was so adamant against it and so insistent that I was allowing the devil into our friendship that I finally compromised on the word of the Lord. I reasoned that perhaps the Holy Ghost was just trying to warn me of an assignment against our friendship. This seemed to satisfy everyone, for no one wants to consider losing a close friend, even for a season.

Well, lo and behold six months later the season of separation began. And it was much more painful and messy than it needed to be. See, the Lord in His kindness and compassion was trying to warn me of what was ahead, not so that I could resist the devil in it. It wasn't the devil orchestrating the separation. It was

God Himself maneuvering to bring a change and take me out of what I didn't realize was a very unhealthy and even abusive setting. When it happened, I initially tried to resist the change. That only left me frustrated, worn out and upset. Then it dawned on me that this was that which the Holy Ghost had spoken. This was the season of separation.

It took some time, but I was able to ease into that season by God's grace. But it didn't need to be so hard. See, the Holy Ghost told me what was going to happen six months ahead of time so that I could prepare myself for the separation and handle it appropriately when it came. But instead, I allowed the voice of man to influence me in a different direction, and it caused great pain.

The Holy Ghost leads and guides us into all truth (John 16:13). But it's not just the major truths of the Word of God that He reveals. He'll lead and guide us into the truth of which restaurant not to visit that night or which road not to turn down the next morning. He knows that the restaurant is overcrowded and the road is congested. He doesn't want us to waste our time. He wants us to redeem it (Ephesians 5:16). So expect to hear His voice, or receive that inner witness, on things big and small—and then don't stop there. Follow Him. There's no need in bragging about how we hear the voice of the Lord if we aren't going to obey what He tells us. Amen?

Beware of False Prophets

Of course, there are also false prophets. Jesus warned of false prophets several times, and so did the New

Testament apostles. We also know false prophets ran rampant in the Old Testament. I imagine there will be false prophets—tares growing up with the wheat—until Jesus comes back. That makes it evermore important to judge prophecy—and to learn how to recognize false prophets. Consider a few of the warnings about false prophets in the New Testament.

> Beware of false prophets, which come to you in sheep's clothing, but inwardly they are ravening wolves.
>
> — Matthew 7:15

I like the Message Bible translation on this one:

> Be wary of false preachers who smile a lot, dripping with practiced sincerity. Chances are they are out to rip you off some way or other. Don't be impressed with charisma; look for character. Who preachers are is the main thing, not what they say. A genuine leader will never exploit your emotions or your pocketbook. These diseased trees with their bad apples are going to be chopped down and burned.
>
> — Matthew 7:15

The Apostle Peter warned of false prophets and false teachers. Peter wrote these words about 2,000 years ago, and we still see false prophets and false teachers running around the Body of Christ today—and believers are still falling into the snare.

> But there were false prophets also among the people, even as there shall be false teachers among you, who privily shall bring in damnable heresies, even denying the Lord that bought them, and bring upon themselves swift destruction.
>
> And many shall follow their pernicious ways; by reason of whom the way of truth shall be evil spoken of.
>
> And through covetousness shall they with feigned words make merchandise of you: whose judgment now of a long time lingereth not, and their damnation slumbereth not.
>
> – 2 Peter 1:1-3

The Apostle Paul also warned of false apostles. You see false apostles today also offering false prophetic utterances that lead the sheep astray:

> For such men are false apostles [spurious, counterfeits], deceitful workmen, masquerading as apostles (special messengers) of Christ (the Messiah). And it is no wonder, for Satan himself

masquerades as an angel of light; So it is not surprising if his servants also masquerade as ministers of righteousness. [But] their end will correspond with their deeds.

— 2 Corinthians 11:13-15 AMP

Some have shied away from prophecy because it is fallible. But there is no reason to be scared of prophecy, prophets or prophetic people. Yes, some error has crept into some circles of the prophetic ministry and no prophet is 100 percent accurate all the time. But God's thoughts toward you are good thoughts. So we should welcome true prophetic words from the Lord. We just have to judge them responsibly rather than throwing out the baby with the defiled bathwater.

The Bible says, "Let the prophets speak two or three, and let the other judge" (1 Corinthians 14:29). If there were no chance that the prophet was missing it, then there wouldn't be any need to judge the word, right?

If you haven't read the preface to this book, please go back and do that now. It offers important information that you need to understand before proceeding to the other 26 ways to judge prophecy.

CHAPTER 2

DOES THE PROPHECY GLORIFY JESUS?

But when he, the Spirit of truth, comes, he will guide you into all truth ... He will bring glory to me by taking from what is mine and making it known to you.

— John 16:13-14

Shortly before Jesus was crucified, He began teaching His disciples about the Holy Spirit. Jesus said His leaving was "profitable" for the apostles because the Holy Spirit—the Comforter, Counselor, Advocate, Intercessor, Strengthener and Standby—could not come into close fellowship with them until He ascended to the right hand of the Father (John 16:7). Jesus promised to send the Holy Spirit to believers once He returned to heaven. Let's listen in:

> But when he, the Spirit of truth, comes, he will guide you into all truth. He will not speak on his own; he will speak only what he hears, and he will tell you what is

yet to come. He will bring glory to me by taking from what is mine and making it known to you. All that belongs to the Father is mine. That is why I said the Spirit will take from what is mine and make it known to you.

– John 16:13-15

Jesus is the Word made flesh. And the Holy Spirit always glorifies the Christ. If the prophetic word does not glorify Christ, then it did not originate from the Holy Spirit. If it did not originate from the Holy Spirit, then it is not of God. If the prophetic word exalts the prophet, then the prophetic word is not from God. Likewise, if it exalts the one receiving the prophetic word, then it is not from God. Hear me on this: If the prophetic word exalts angels, it is not from God. The Holy Ghost is in the business of exalting Jesus, not the ones serving Him.

You Are My Wife! But I'm Already Married!

You've probably heard prophecies that promise babies and husbands. Maybe you've even received one. I am not against such prophetic words, per se, but I believe any prophet who prophesies directional words about husbands and babies needs to be especially cautious. Prophets acting in presumption have caused plenty of damage to relationships and the hearts of love-seeking people. One minister shared two examples of such prophecies. Both were questionable and both turned out to be false. Let's listen to Jackie's story:

"The prophet told me I was his wife, which wouldn't have been such a big issue if I weren't already someone else's wife! The prophet also told me that God was answering my prayer for weight loss and he saw me as a size two. That's not even my bone structure or desire at all. Another prophet told me God was giving me the car of my dreams—a white convertible. I absolutely do not like convertibles or white cars! And I had countless pregnancy prophecies in 2007 that I would conceive that year. Well, it's 2010 and no baby!"

Thank God, this woman knew how to judge prophecy and didn't get false hopes up or go chasing possessions.

Now let me give you the other side of the prophetic coin. Prophets can indeed prophesy true prophetic words about marriage. A brother named Michael shared with me how a prophet told him on a several different occasions that he would be getting married. "I told him that is the last thing I would even want. My first marriage was akin to a horror movie. My wife was unfaithful," Michael explained. "But now I am happily married two months and loving it." It was apparently God's will for this young man to marry again. Even though his soul was gun shy over a bad experience in his first marriage, God appears to have arranged circumstances in his life that led him to a loving wife—even though his soul didn't initially agree with the prophetic word.

Directional prophecy can also be lifesaving. Mary tells the story of how she and her husband were seeking the Lord about a new job. The following is an example of things not always looking as they appear.

> "All of a sudden my husband's father asked him to join him in a business in another state. We were excited and thought that may be the direction to take. A prophet was at our church and asked us both to stand up. He told us the Lord said to stay where we were and not to move. In a few months we found out my mom had a terminal disease. I was the closest one to take care of her. God knew what we needed—a timely word to change our course. My mom got saved in that same time period before she passed."

Glory to God! Thank God for prophetic ministry! And thank God for this couple's ability to rightly judge the prophetic word and act on it.

Prophesying Judgment

Let me give you another illustration of how a prophetic word can glorify the prophet instead of Jesus, making it questionable. If a prophet prophesies that judgment will come upon a city unless the mayor takes heed to his advice, then that prophetic word exalts the prophet. If a prophet tells you that your gifts have been so misunderstood, then prophesies that the Lord is going to deal with the ones who have held you back, that glorifies the one receiving the prophecy. Can you see how neither one of those examples glorifies God? Yes,

God will exalt us in due season when we humble ourselves under His mighty hand. And God may even choose fit to have a prophet prophesy a coming promotion in the spirit. But the Holy Spirit is not going to puff you up by putting others down. Flattery is the domain of Jezebel spirits.

Increasing Your Vision

Sometimes prophetic words take us by surprise. God is able to do immeasurably more than all we ask or imagine, according to His power that is at work within us (Ephesians 3:20 NIV). Ally tells me the story of a prophetic utterance that didn't make perfect sense to her soul, but rang true in her spirit—and came true indeed.

> "We are pastors. We were visiting a church and received a prophetic word that specifically said God was sending His sons and daughters from afar to sit and receive from our ministry. Three weeks later we heard God's voice say to start a Spanish church. We were a little surprised since we spoke no Spanish but we did it. God did it and today the church is 300 strong! The prophetic word came before the personal confirming word from God in our hearts. It increased our vision."

Ally's prophecy also glorified God. So, remember, the Holy Spirit will bring glory to Jesus by taking from what is His and making it known to you (John 16).

CHAPTER 3

DOES THE PROHECY AGREE WITH SCRIPTURE?

For there are three that bear record in heaven, the Father, the Word, and the Holy Ghost: and these three are one.

— 1 John 5:7

The Holy Ghost doesn't contradict Himself. Let me say that again. The Holy Ghost doesn't contradict Himself. If the Holy Spirit inspired the Scriptures—and He did—then why would the Holy Spirit speak something that directly contradicts what He inspired? Of course, the answer is clear: He wouldn't. He's not schizophrenic.

The Holy Ghost doesn't speak with a forked tongue. That's the domain of Satan, the serpent. It's the Devil who tempts you to sin and then torments you after you do. The Holy Spirit convicts you of sin so you can receive forgiveness when you confess it.

What am I saying? If the prophetic word flies in the face of the written Word, then you need to let it keep flying right out the window. Don't receive it. But also be careful of people twisting Scripture in the name of a rhema word from heaven. Here's an example: "The Spirit says to sow $638 so you can manifest a tenfold return on your seed according to Luke 6:38." Luke 6:38 says give and it shall be given to you, good measure, pressed down, shaken together, and running over, shall men give into your bosom.

I have never seen anything in the written Word of God—no principle, no precept, and no pattern—where God plays a wild numbers game with money to get you a blessing. The fact of the matter is, you can put your faith on the Scripture itself and believe God for the manifestation of His promise—giving according to how the Holy Spirit leads you as an individual.

Apparently, I'm not the only one in the Body of Christ to witness this false prophetic numbers game. Many have written to tell me their story of how prophets connected God's manifest blessing to specific dollar amounts. Here's one of the many that come to mind: A certain prophet told a believer named Theresa to send him $150 for the reconciliation of a relationship—in U.S. dollars. (Apparently, God doesn't accept pesos.) Thank God that Theresa knew better. But what if she had followed the false prophetic directive and sent the money? It would have been a total waste. God doesn't charge for reconciliation. Jesus already paid that price and He gives man a free will to choose.

Giving Prompted by the Heart

When God set out to build a tabernacle so He could dwell among the Israelites, He told Moses this: "Tell the Israelites to bring me an offering. You are to receive the offering for me from each man whose heart prompts him to give" (Exodus 25:2 NIV). Giving is a heart issue. The widow with the mite would be out of luck in some churches today because she couldn't afford to buy her way out of poverty by tapping into a televised prophetic numbers game. But God looks at the heart. Prophecies that put pressure on you to do something that contradicts the Word, whether in the matter of giving or anything else, should be rejected.

Inspired by the Holy Spirit, the Apostle John wrote, "For there are three that bear record in heaven, the Father, the Word, and the Holy Ghost: and these three are one" (1 John 5:7). Father, Son and Holy Ghost are in perfect unity. Therefore, Jesus (the Word) will always agree with the Holy Ghost and the Holy Ghost will always agree with the Father and the Father will always agree with Jesus. If the prophecy does not agree with the Word, it didn't come from the Holy Spirit.

CHAPTER 4
DOES THE PROPHECY POINT YOU TO JESUS?

No flesh should glory in his presence.

– 1 John 5:7

Just as true prophetic words glorify Jesus Christ, the head of the Church, true prophetic words should point you toward Jesus for the grace to walk it out. Apart from Him, we can do nothing (John 15:5). "Nothing" includes manifesting a prophetic word in our lives.

When we receive a true prophetic word, it is God's expressed will for us—but He's not going to allow us to rely on ourselves, on a prophetic messenger, or on anybody else to bring a prophetic word to pass. The proper response to a prophetic word is surrender and reliance on Jesus, the Author and Finisher of our faith. God is the One who authored the prophetic word. God is the One who gives us faith to believe the prophetic word. And God is the One who gives us the strength and strategies to walk into the manifestation of the prophetic word.

Angels Are Fellow Servants

With this truth in mind, prophets and prophetic words should point you toward Jesus. It's tempting to exalt the prophetic messenger, but the Apostle John was corrected when he made the mistake of worshipping the prophetic messenger rather than the One who authored the prophetic message he received on the Isle of Patmos.

> Then [the angel] said to me, Write this down: Blessed (happy, to be envied) are those who are summoned (invited, called) to the marriage supper of the Lamb. And he said to me [further], These are the true words (the genuine and exact declarations) of God. Then I fell prostrate at his feet to worship (to pay divine honors) to him, but he [restrained me] and said, Refrain! [You must not do that!] I am [only] another servant with you and your brethren who have [accepted and hold] the testimony borne by Jesus. Worship God! For the substance (essence) of the truth revealed by Jesus is the spirit of all prophecy [the vital breath, the inspiration of all inspired preaching and interpretation of the divine will and purpose, including both mine and yours].
>
> – Revelation 19:9-10 (AMP)

Prophets are fellow servants. Like the angel John encountered, prophets—and the prophetic words they deliver—should honor Jesus. Beware of prophets who do otherwise. Although this book is not about recognizing false prophets, Jesus did warn about the motives of those who speak on their own authority.

> He who speaks on his own authority seeks to win honor for himself. [He whose teaching originates with himself seeks his own glory.] But He Who seeks the glory and is eager for the honor of Him Who sent Him, He is true; and there is no unrighteousness or falsehood or deception in Him.
>
> – John 7:18 AMP

When someone prophesies, it should be by the authority of Jesus Christ and by the unction of the Holy Ghost, not the authority of his imagination and the unction of his ulterior motives. A prophet's authority comes from Jesus Christ. The true prophetic word comes from the Holy Spirit. If the Spirit of God said that, then it should lead you to the feet of Jesus to thank Him for His good plan and receive grace to pursue it. If the prophetic messenger isn't pointing you to Jesus, it should send up a red flag in your spirit. Jesus is the Truth. He is the Word. Apart from Him we can do nothing.

Confused About Marriage Prophecy

Mary is still confused and crying out to God for understanding over prophecies she received about an impending marriage to a certain man of God. You can literally hear the hurt and disappointment in her letter. As you read it, consider whether or not the prophetic word exalted Jesus.

"I was told about a year and a half ago by a professed prophet that I was getting ready to be married and that the man of God was very close to me. He then told me to turn and kiss the air because that's just how close he was to me. I was a little skeptical so he asked me if I believed he was a prophet.

"Funny thing is this ... At that time I was in a relationship with a man that I thought could definitely be my soul mate. I absolutely had no other men in my life. A few months later, the relationship appeared to be progressing rapidly. He even paid for me to go on a trip to visit my family out of state. I thought he was going to pop the question.

"Well that didn't happen, as a matter of fact when I returned he disappeared out of my life. What's even more baffling is that I had received several more prophetic words around that same time and throughout that relationship through my pastor and others. All of the prophetic words declared that I was getting ready to be married. I even people telling me to start buying lingerie and things for my house, because it was getting ready to happen soon.

"Even though I operate in the prophetic too, I'm still trying to make sense of it all. The man I thought I would marry has been gone out of my life almost a year now and there isn't anybody else in my life. I pray that I can get understanding with all this because I still question whether any of it was God."

How to Counsel Mary

What can we say to Mary? It's possible that these prophets and pastors were tapping into the idolatry in Mary's heart. Now, I don't know Mary or if that's the case. But when prophetic words don't come to pass, the reason could be that it wasn't really God's will, but God allowed the prophet to prophesy out of the idolatry in the person's heart (Ezekiel 14:4). We'll discuss that more in the next chapter.

Of course, it's also possible that the man with whom Mary was in relationship is the man of God mentioned in the prophetic word and that he did not obey God. It's also possible that the man of God in the prophetic word was an Ishmael. In other words, perhaps God is sending Mary a husband, a man of God that's close to her who she hasn't even considered, who she isn't even dating, and who she wouldn't even think was a candidate. It's possible that God will open her eyes and it will all make sense.

It's also possible that "soon" means something different to men than it does to God. To God, a day is like a thousand years and a thousand years is like a day. If the timing of a prophetic word is not explicit (three weeks from now, within the next year, by this time tomorrow, etc.) it can sometimes be difficult to discern. In those cases, we just trust God for His perfect will in His perfect time and continue seeking the Kingdom of God and His righteousness.

Now that we've considered all of those possibilities about Mary's situation, we need to consider one more: it's very possible that the prophecies were just plain wrong. It's possible that one prophet missed it and the others who heard the prophecy kept repeating the prophetic word because they hoped it was true. Sometimes when people in a body hear a prophetic word they like, you'll hear variations of that word announced that become "confirmation." But just because five—or even 500—people prophesy the same thing doesn't mean God said that. You still have to judge the word.

Mary needs to be equipped to judge prophecy so that she can discern what is what for herself. She flows in the prophetic, but she is still confused about this prophecy. She is still seeking answers from God. She is still not sure. Mary seemed to have wanted this man of God to pop the question. She seemed disappointed when he didn't. What she needs right now more than anything is to understand God's will for her life and exalt Jesus. The repeated prophecies about a "soon" marriage in her life didn't cause her to exalt Jesus. They left her confused. God is not the author of confusion (1 Corinthians 14:33). The Spirit bears witness with our spirit.

CHAPTER 5

DOES THE PROPHECY LEAD YOU INTO IDOLATRY?

Wherefore, my dearly beloved, flee from idolatry.

– 1 Corinthians 10:13

If a prophetic word causes you to chase after other gods, then the Spirit of God did not say that. Even if prophecy is presented with signs and wonders coming to pass that is not proof the Spirit of God said it—and if it leads you into idolatry you can be sure He didn't say it. So let's be clear about what is an idol and what is idolatry before we go any further.

The simplest definition of "idol" is a false god. Merriam-Webster defines idol as a "representation or symbol of an object of worship; a false god. Another definition is "pretender, impostor." Yet another definition is "an object of extreme devotion" or "a false conception."

In ancient times, people created wooden, silver and golden idols and assigned them names that represented specific gods. Today, we are a little more sophisticated and the enemy is a little subtler. We would never dream of worshipping a golden calf. But we may be tempted to worship our favorite sport, our career, or our children. In other words, we may unconsciously set up people, places and things as idols in our lives—and those idols draw our attention away from God. Anything that draws our attention away from God is a pretender and an imposter. Any object of extreme devotion apart from God is a false God.

Hear this: Even our own hurts and wounds can become like idols. This can happen when the time and energy we should spend focusing on God is spent focusing on our wounds. Yes, healing is a process. But if we aren't careful we can get out of balance and give that hurt too much power in our lives. Our focus needs to be on the God who can heal the hurt. Sometimes, we don't want to give up the hurt because we feel justified. So we cater to it. We serve it. We build walls to keep people from touching it. And in doing so we may miss opportunities to do the will of God. Selah. Pause and think about that for a moment.

Idolatry, then, is the worship of a physical object as a God, or the immoderate attachment or devotion to something. It could be just about anything—and it's not godly. The Bible clearly says, "You shall have no other gods before me" (Exodus 20:3). In case you didn't hear it right in Exodus, the Holy Spirit repeats Himself in Deuteronomy 5:7: "You shall have no other gods before me." And once more, "For thou shalt worship no other god: for the Lord, whose name is Jealous, is a jealous God" (Exodus 34:14).

Prophecy and Idolatry

Now that we understand idols and idolatry, let's look at how we can use this understanding to judge prophecy. Let's go straight to the Word of God, where we can clearly connect the two.

> If there arise among you a prophet, or a dreamer of dreams, and giveth thee a sign or a wonder, And the sign or the wonder come to pass, whereof he spake unto thee, saying, Let us go after other gods, which thou hast not known, and let us serve them; Thou shalt not hearken unto the words of that prophet, or that dreamer of dreams: for the Lord your God proveth you, to know whether ye love the Lord your God with all your heart and with all your soul. Ye shall walk after the Lord your God, and fear him, and keep his commandments, and obey his voice, and ye shall serve him, and cleave unto him. And that prophet, or that dreamer of dreams, shall be put to death; because he hath spoken to turn you away from the Lord your God, which brought you out of the land of Egypt, and redeemed you out of the house of bondage, to thrust thee out of the way which the Lord thy God commanded thee to walk in. So shalt thou put the evil away from the midst of thee.

> — Deuteronomy 13:1-5

In the Old Covenant, a prophet that led people to other gods got the death sentence. We're in a time of grace today, so we can't judge a prophecy by waiting to see if something unfortunate befalls the prophet who released the word. The point here is to show you that true prophetic utterances won't lead you to serve other gods.

Practical Idolatry

Let me give you a practical example. A prophet prophesied that Jim was about to get a promotion on his job. But the prophetic word came with a caveat. In order to get the promotion, Jim will need to put in longer hours and submit to his hard-hearted boss. Jim is excited about the promotion because his heart's desire is to earn more money, have a better title, gain the esteem of his peers, and so on. So he decides to walk out the prophetic word.

But did the Spirit of God really say that? You be the judge. Here's what happened next: Jim's unsaved boss started insisting that he work nights and weekends for the next few months to catch up on a big order. This puts stress on Jim's family and causes him to miss church. It brings imbalance and instability in Jim's life, but his desire for the promotion—and the apparent confirmation of the prophetic word—causes him to ignore the warning signs from his wife, his pastor and his own physical body, which is exhausted. After the big project is complete, Jim doesn't get the promotion and he's got a mess at home. Jim wore himself out because he was in the flesh instead of the grace of God as he chased after his idol.

Matthew 6:33 says, "Seek first the kingdom of God, and his righteousness; and all these things shall be added unto you." The New Living Translation puts it this way: "Seek the Kingdom of God above all else, and live righteously, and he will give you everything you need." The Message Bible translates it, "Steep your life in God-reality, God-initiative, God-provisions. Don't worry about missing out. You'll find all your everyday human concerns will be met."

Flee From Idolatry

Matthew makes it pretty clear, huh? We aren't to seek idols. We are to seek God. The psalmist said, "Trust in the Lord and do good; dwell in the land and enjoy safe pasture. Delight yourself in the Lord and he will give you the desires of your heart" (Psalm 37:3-4).

If you get a prophecy about a promotion, a marriage, an increased anointing—or whatever—don't seek after the promotion, the marriage, the anointing, or the gift. Seek after the God, the Giver of the gift. You'll never go wrong that way. God will get you what you are supposed to have when you put Him first.

In his first letter to the church at Corinth, Paul gave some important instructions to the saints. He said, "Wherefore, my dearly beloved, flee from idolatry" (1 Corinthians 10:14). The Amplified Bible trumpets the warning even louder and even clearer: "Therefore, my dearly beloved, shun (keep clear away from, avoid by flight if need be) any sort of idolatry (of loving or venerating anything more than God)."

"Flee" is a strong word. Mirriam-Webster's dictionary defines "flee" as to run away, often from danger or evil; to hurry toward a place of security. Idolatry is a dangerous thing.

It's always possible that you received true prophetic word and you made an idol of the thing. The prophet was spot on, but your heart isn't right. That is a work of the flesh that Paul the Apostle outlined in his letter to the Galatians.

> Now the works of the flesh are manifest, which are these; Adultery, fornication, uncleanness, lasciviousness, Idolatry, witchcraft, hatred, variance, emulations, wrath, strife, seditions, heresies, Envyings, murders, drunkenness, revellings, and such like: of the which I tell you before, as I have also told you in time past, that they which do such things shall not inherit the kingdom of God.
>
> – Galatians 5:19-21

So again, does the prophetic word lead you into idolatry? If it does, it's probably not of God. Even if it is a true word from God and you make it into an idol, God is liable to wait until you wear yourself out and turn back to Him. Apart from Him, we can do nothing. And no flesh shall glory in His presence (1 Corinthians 1:29).

CHAPTER 6

DOES THE PROPHECY TRY TO ESTABLISH NEW DOCTRINE?

If any man will do his will, he shall know of the doctrine, whether it be of God, or whether I speak of myself.

— 1 Corinthians 10:13

The New Testament has plenty to say about doctrine. What is doctrine? Doctrine, quite literally, means teaching or instruction. Merriam-Webster also defines doctrine as "a principle or position or body of principles in a branch of knowledge or system of belief."

The doctrines of Christ, for example, are clear. Jesus teaches us to love God, and to love our neighbors as we love ourselves. Jesus teaches us to be meek. Jesus teaches us to forgive and show mercy, and so on. The epistles are Holy Spirit-inspired letters that expound on the practical aspects of the doctrines of Christ as they relate to Church government, giving, submission to authority, relationships and so on.

If a prophetic word strays from the foundations of the doctrines of Christ, seeking to establish new doctrine, it is either a doctrine of men (Colossians 2:22) or a doctrine of devils (1 Timothy 4:1). The Apostle Paul warned the Church about the dangers of both because they cause us to depart from faith and grace.

Although prophets do receive new revelations, prophets should not be attempting to establish new doctrine that leads men into the bondage of legalism or into the fellowship of seducing spirits. The doctrines of Christ offer the truth that set us free. Any other doctrines bind our liberty. When you think about how many cults have formed and how many lives have been destroyed based on some "new doctrine," the danger becomes clear.

Beware Erroneous Doctrine

The Bible repeatedly warns of erroneous doctrine. In the Book of Jeremiah, the prophet speaks of doctrines of vanities (Jeremiah 10:8). The Amplified Bible translation puts it this way:

Who would not fear You, O King of the nations? For it is fitting to You and Your due! For among all the wise [men or gods] of the nations and in all their kingdoms, there is none like You. But they are altogether irrational and stupid and foolish. Their instruction is given by idols who are but wood [it is a teaching of falsity, emptiness, futility]!

– Jeremiah 10:7-8 (AMP)

Can you imagine receiving instruction for living from idols? Sad to say, some Christians do. No, they may not exalt a wooden statue—or even a solid gold statute. But they may exalt a person who is teaching error, or demonic imaginations that lead them to the fringes of the Word of God, or seducing spirits that take them completely out of sound doctrine into falsity, emptiness and futility.

Jesus Himself warned of the doctrines of commandments of men, even suggesting that those who teach man-made ideas as commands from God are not close to the heart of God.

> This people draweth nigh unto me with their mouth, and honoureth me with their lips; but their heart is far from me. But in vain they do worship me, teaching for doctrines the commandments of men.
>
> – Matthew 15:8-9

Prophets must be close to the heart of God to speak from the heart of God. It's a scary proposition, then, to consider prophesying or submitting to newfangled doctrines of men. It leads to religious error at best.

Did Jesus Have a New Doctrine?

The Pharisees and the Saducees—examples of the religious spirit—saddled Israel with thousands of man-made laws that were diametrically opposed to the spirit of the law. Remember, the Word and the Spirit agree. When you hear a prophetic word that goes against the grain of the written Word of God as it attempts to establish new doctrine, chalk it up as a false prophecy.

The multitudes were astonished at Jesus' doctrine (Matthew 22:23; Mark 1:22) and some even thought it was new doctrine (Mark 1:27), but Jesus was fulfilling the true intent of the Scriptures. The doctrine of Jesus has power (Luke 4:32) and the words that He speaks are spirit and life.

So how do you tell if the doctrine is really of God? Keeping your heart clean and being a student of the Word will help you avoid false doctrines. Jesus said His doctrine came from the Father, and added:

> If any man will do his will, he shall know of the doctrine, whether it be of God, or whether I speak of myself.
>
> – John 7:17

Here are two cues you can take from Jesus: seek after God's will and examine the fruit of the prophet.

The Amplified translation of Verse 17 says that if any one desires to do God's pleasure, he will know—he will have the needed illumination to recognize, and can tell for himself—whether the teaching is from God.

Prophetic Alignment

Where we get into trouble is when our will is not completely aligned with the will of God in a matter. It goes back to idolatry. When we want something (anything) more than God's will, we tend to believe what we want to believe rather than what God tells us to believe. That's deception. When we set our heart's to God's will no matter what our soul or flesh tells us, we'll better discern whether a teaching or a prophetic word is from God or man.

True five-fold ministers labor to ensure believers are established in sound doctrine.

> And he gave some, apostles; and some, prophets; and some, evangelists; and some, pastors and teachers; For the perfecting of the saints, for the work of the ministry, for the edifying of the body of Christ: Till we all come in the unity of the faith, and of the knowledge of the Son of God, unto a perfect man, unto the measure of the stature of the fulness of Christ: That we henceforth be no more children, tossed to and fro, and carried about with every wind of doctrine, by the sleight of men, and cunning craftiness, whereby they lie in wait to deceive; But speaking the truth in love, may grow up into him in all things, which is the head, even Christ.

> – Ephesians 4:11-15

One true five-fold minister, the Apostle Paul, offered no wiggle room when dealing with people who tried to introduce doctrines out of line with the revealed Word of God in Scripture. Let's listen in to his Holy Ghost instruction so we can get an even deeper understanding of how serious it is when prophetic ministers release utterances that seek to establish new doctrine.

> Now I beseech you, brethren, mark them which cause divisions and offences contrary to the doctrine which ye have learned; and avoid them.
>
> For they that are such serve not our Lord Jesus Christ, but their own belly; and by good words and fair speeches deceive the hearts of the simple.
>
> — Romans 16:17-18

Paul didn't advise us to merely spit out the sticks of prophecy that doesn't agree with the doctrines of Christ. He urgently and anxiously begged believers in Rome to mark and avoid them as people who serve other gods and seek to deceive. That's how serious is the matter of trying to establish new doctrine. Indeed, it could have eternal consequences.

Although there is a difference between false doctrine and doctrines of devils (someone preaching false doctrine may not be purposely trying to deceive anyone and may change their course if corrected) false doctrine is nonetheless false and should not be accepted in any manner in which it is delivered.

Consider Paul's advice to Timothy, and consider how this applies to the prophetic.

> If anyone teaches a different doctrine and does not agree with the sound words of our Lord Jesus Christ and the teaching that accords with godliness, he is puffed up with conceit and understands nothing. He has an unhealthy craving for controversy and for quarrels about words, which produce envy, dissension, slander, evil suspicions, and constant friction among people who are depraved in mind and deprived of the truth, imagining that godliness is a means of gain.
>
> – 1 Timothy 6:3-5

CHAPTER 7

DOES THE PROPHET ACKNOWLEDGE CHRIST'S LORDSHIP?

They profess to know God, but they deny him by their works. They are detestable, disobedient, unfit for any good work.

— Titus 1:16

Does the prophet acknowledge the Lordship of Christ? At its surface, that may seem like a strange question. Who would let someone in their pulpit who wasn't walking with the Lord? It happens. In today's age, itinerant ministers are sometimes invited to preach based on the crowds they draw rather than a relationship that would offer insight into their character.

In his first letter to the Corinthian church, Paul spent considerable time addressing spiritual gifts, including prophetic words. Let's listen in:

Now concerning spiritual gifts, brethren, I would not have you ignorant. Ye know that ye were Gentiles, carried away unto these dumb idols, even as ye were led.

Wherefore I give you to understand, that no man speaking by the Spirit of God calleth Jesus accursed: and that no man can say that Jesus is the Lord, but by the Holy Ghost.

Now there are diversities of gifts, but the same Spirit. And there are differences of administrations, but the same Lord. And there are diversities of operations, but it is the same God which worketh all in all. But the manifestation of the Spirit is given to every man to profit withal. For to one is given by the Spirit the word of wisdom; to another the word of knowledge by the same Spirit;

To another faith by the same Spirit; to another the gifts of healing by the same Spirit; To another the working of miracles; to another prophecy; to another discerning of spirits; to another divers kinds of tongues; to another the interpretation of tongues: But all these worketh that one and the selfsame Spirit, dividing to every man severally as he will.

– 1 Corinthians 12:1-11

As Spirit-filled believers, we like to understand the manifestations of the Spirit. We love to flow in words of wisdom and words of knowledge. We enjoy witnessing gifts of healing and working of miracles. We covet prophecy and so on. But Paul peppered in some important points we need to pay close attention to in any discussion of spiritual gifts.

First, Paul made it clear that he doesn't want us to be ignorant about spiritual gifts. The Amplified Bible says "uninformed." When we are ignorant about how the Word works and how the Spirit works, we are prone to deception. When we are misinformed about spiritual gifts, we are liable to be led astray—away from the Lordship of Christ to serving idols.

Before Paul explains the manifestations of the Spirit, he offers a warning. I like how The Message translation puts it because it's very plain:

> Remember how you were when you didn't know God, led from one phony god to another, never knowing what you were doing, just doing it because everybody else did it? It's different in this life. God wants us to use our intelligence, to seek to understand as well as we can. For instance, by using your heads, you know perfectly well that the Spirit of God would never prompt anyone to say "Jesus be damned!" Nor would anyone be inclined to say "Jesus is Master!" without the insight of the Holy Spirit.
>
> – 1 Corinthians 12:2-3 (MSG)

Think about it for a minute. Do you remember how you were when you didn't know God? Well, first of all you weren't under the Lordship of Christ. But interestingly enough, even unbelievers catch on to much of the false prophecy, merchandising and error in the Church. Discerning of spirits is helpful to judge prophecy, but you don't have to be a Bible scholar (and some don't even have to be born again) to discern that something is just "off."

It's common sense that no one who is led by the Spirit of God would curse Jesus. But when prophets curse God's people, they aren't acknowledging the Lordship of Jesus Christ. The Word of God admonishes us to bless and curse not (Romans 12:14). Therefore, to curse is to rebel against the head of the Church, the Lordship of Christ.

Christ redeemed us from the curse of the Law by becoming a curse for us (Galatians 3:13). Guess what? Jesus didn't come to curse unbelievers, either. The Bible is crystal clear when it says, "For God sent not his Son into the world to condemn the world; but that the world through him might be saved" (John 3:17). Let's drive the point home with the Message Translation:

> This is how much God loved the world: He gave his Son, his one and only Son. And this is why: so that no one need be destroyed; by believing in him, anyone can have a whole and lasting life. God didn't go to all the trouble of sending his Son

merely to point an accusing finger, telling the world how bad it was. He came to help, to put the world right again. Anyone who trusts in him is acquitted; anyone who refuses to trust him has long since been under the death sentence without knowing it. And why? Because of that person's failure to believe in the one-of-a-kind Son of God when introduced to him.

– John 3:17-19

Once again, prophecy should acknowledge the Lordship of Christ. Curses don't fit into that truth. Yet I hear so many prophetic curses being released over peoples and nations. I don't bear witness to those prophecies because they don't line up with the Word.

Another way that prophecies can fail to acknowledge the Lordship of Christ is by exalting angels above their due position. The writer of Hebrews explained, "Are not all angels ministering spirits sent to serve those who will inherit salvation?" (Hebrews 1:14)

Angels are here to serve us, not the other way around. By the same token, angels only have the power and authority that God gives them. Without being empowered by the Word of God, angels are restricted in their function. So any prophecy that exalts angels is erroneous. We've seen plenty of this in the Body of Christ as well. Keep in mind that there are evil angels that seek to deceive. They are called demons and Satan is their Lord.

Let no man beguile you of your reward in a voluntary humility and worshipping of angels, intruding into those things which he hath not seen, vainly puffed up by his fleshly mind, And not holding the Head, from which all the body by joints and bands having nourishment ministered, and knit together, increaseth with the increase of God.

– Colossians 2:18-19

When we exalt angels, we aren't acknowledging the Lordship of Christ. That's plain and simple. When we exalt idols in any form, we aren't acknowledging the Lordship of Christ.

The Angel Says, "Stop Praying!"

A man named Jordan sent me a message about a strange prophecy concerning directives from angels. While God can use angels as prophetic messengers, the message they deliver should still bear witness with the written Word of God and our spirit. Arlie writes, "A supposed man of God, a pastor, said an angel told him to tell us that we were to stop praying, that God had heard our prayer and was going to save our friends and family. I did swallow it for a second!"

Who would want you to stop praying for the salvation of your loved ones? An angel of light or an angel of darkness? Here's the point: if God gives you a release in your spirit, you can stop praying. But consider Daniel, who fasted and prayed for 21 days. The angels were warring in the heavenlies to get the answer to Daniel. What if he had stopped praying before the answer manifested? What if one of the principalities and powers came to Daniel's buddies and told him, "Tell Danny to stop praying. God already heard him and He's going to answer the prayer."

Again, I'm not saying that God can't send an angel as a messenger. I'm just saying there has been a lot of error around angels in the prophetic and I wouldn't bet my family's salvation on a prophet who said an angel told him I could stop interceding.

Paul's Prophetic Conclusion

At the beginning of this chapter, we looked at Paul's words in 1 Corinthians 12. He began talking about spiritual gifts, including the gifts of prophecy, with a warning not to be ignorant. Paul continues teaching throughout the next two chapters and concludes with this:

> If any man think himself to be a prophet, or spiritual, let him acknowledge that the things that I write unto you are the commandments of the Lord. But if any man be ignorant, let him be ignorant. Wherefore, brethren, covet to prophesy, and forbid not to speak with tongues. Let all things be done decently and in order.
>
> – 1 Corinthians 14:36-39

Doing things decently and in order means always acknowledging the Lordship of Christ. Bottom line.

Let me leave you with one last thought: Just because a minister exalts Christ in his worship or even his message—even if a minister casts out devils in the name of Jesus—that doesn't mean his prophetic utterances are true. You can't buy into prophetic words just because everything around the prophetic word looks good. You still have to judge it. All prophecy, no matter from whom it comes, must be judged.

PART TWO
THE FRUIT-BASED TESTS

For every one that useth milk is unskilful in the word of
righteousness: for he is a babe. But strong meat belongeth to them
that are of full age, even those who by reason of use have their
senses exercised to discern both good and evil.

– Hebrews 5:13-14

The ultimate test of a prophetic word is the written Word of God. Although this book is organized in parts that aim to make it easier to train the senses to discern both good and evil, the entire manuscript points back to the Word of God as a witness.

In Part Two of this book, we'll explore what I call the Fruit-Based Tests. What is the fruit of the prophetic word? What does it produce in your life? Fear? Control? Peace? Comfort? Stability? Instability? Always remember this: He that prophesieth speaketh unto men to edification, and exhortation, and comfort (1 Corinthians 14:3).

If the fruit of a prophetic word doesn't fit into those categories, you should question the source. Yes, there are true rebukes of the Spirit. There are dire warnings. There are challenging directive words. But these are the exception rather than the rule, especially when it comes to personal prophecy. A prophecy that puts you under a curse is not of God.

So with a continued focus on the written Word of God, let's continue in part two with an exploration of the Fruit-Based tests.

CHAPTER 8

DO THE PROPHECIES COME TO PASS?

We do not want you to become lazy, but to imitate those who through faith and patience inherit what has been promised.

– Hebrews 6:12 (NIV)

In the Old Testament, the test of prophecy was pretty cut and dried: Did it come to pass? That helps on the back end of the matter, but what did they do while they were waiting for the prophecy to come to pass?

Sometimes seeing a prophecy come to pass is a matter of faith and patience (and sometimes also preparation on your part). But how can you be sure, or at least relatively sure, that you aren't putting your faith and patience on a prophetic promise that's not from God? How can you be sure that the prophetic word is not merely a distraction from God's actual will?

Let's look at the Scripture.

You may say to yourselves, "How can we know when a message has not been spoken by the Lord?" If what a prophet proclaims in the name of the Lord does not take place or come true, that is a message the Lord has not spoken. That prophet has spoken presumptuously. Do not be afraid of him.

– Deuteronomy 18:21-22

Prophets in the New Testament can also speak presumptuously. What does it literally mean to presume? And what exactly is presumption? When you presume, you form an opinion from little or no evidence. Presumption also means to take as true or as fact without actual proof. "Presumptuous" could also mean "to overstep due bounds" and "to take liberties." Those definitions outline some critical dos and don'ts of prophecy. First, we must be clear that there is no room for personal opinion in the prophetic. Our "proof" must come from the Holy Spirit, not our own spirits or some other spirit. As mouthpieces for God, others take our words and insights very seriously, and we cannot abuse the grace people perceive on our lives.

Presumption Won't Kill You, But it Could Hurt Your Ministry

Doubtless, God hates presumption—and He has good reason. There are several variations of the Greek word "presume." Typically, the word portrays insolence (insultingly contemptuous speech or conduct), pride, arrogance, or audacity (bold or arrogant disregard for normal restraints). Considering that the Lord includes a proud look and a false witness among the His seven abominations, presumption is not something to be taken lightly.

In fact, while the King James Version of the Bible only mentions the words presume, presumed, presumptuous and presumptuously 11 times, the act almost always leads to the death. In my opinion, there are few things worse in the world of church than a presumptuous prophet. Deuteronomy 18:20 declares, "The prophet who presumes to speak a word in my name which I have not commanded him to speak, or who speaks in the name of other gods, the same prophet shall die."

Mercy! Of course, we are living in a time of grace and the presumptuous prophet probably won't be struck dead for this sin. Jesus died for the sin of the world, including our occasional presumptions.

Reputation for Accuracy Not Enough

Alright, now let's get off the bunny trail of presumption and get back to the main thing: Do the prophecies come to pass? What do we do while we are waiting to find out if the prophecy comes to pass?

When we use the test of whether or not a prophet's prophecies come to past, many times we have to look his or her track record of accuracy. Does the prophet have a reputation for prophesying things that come true? Or does the prophet continuously prophesy and none of it ever comes to pass? Or does the prophet's track record fall somewhere between those two extremes?

It's definitely helpful to look at the fruit of the prophet's ministry in terms of accuracy, but this "test" should be used in conjunction with other tests. Put another way, just because a prophet has a track record for being ultra accurate (or by contrast just because a young prophet doesn't have much of an established track record yet) doesn't in itself confirm or invalidate a prophetic word.

A prophet with an accurate track record and abundant fruit in his or her life can certainly miss it. No prophet is infallible because man is not infallible. Alternatively, even a young prophet without much of a history in ministry can be spot on with the Word of the Lord. So although we should look at the fruit of the ministry, again, we can't look at the fruit alone. Consider this Scripture:

> For false Christs and false prophets shall rise, and shall shew signs and wonders, to seduce, if it were possible, even the elect.
>
> – Mark 13:22

What About Conditional Prophecies?

Of course, some prophecies are conditional. God's written Word is chock full of promises that are conditional. So why would a prophetic Word have any different standard?

Conditional promises, whether written or prophetic, are promises where God can't do His part unless we do our part. God won't do our part, but we can't do God's part. Think about it for a minute. Salvation is conditional upon our believing with our hearts and confessing with our mouths that Jesus is Lord. If you draw nigh to God, He will draw nigh to you (James 4:8). If you humble yourself in the sight of the Lord, He will lift you up (James 4:10). Get the picture?

In the same way, prophecies can be conditional. Remember Nineveh? Jonah entered Nineveh and declared, "Yet forty days and Nineveh shall be overthrown" (Jonah 3:4). The people of Nineveh didn't just accept this fate. Instead, some of the people believed God and proclaimed a fast and put on sackcloth in hopes that He would show mercy.

Even the king sat in ashes and encouraged the people to turn away from evil and violence in hopes that God would change His mind. What happened? "And God saw their works, that they turned from their evil way; and God repented of evil that he had said that he would do unto them; and he did it not" (Jonah 3:9-10). Nineveh's salvation was conditional upon repentance.

Let's look, though, at a more practical example. Imagine someone prophesies that you are going to launch into international evangelism. As part of your calling, the genuine prophetic word declares, you will travel to many nations. You will preach the Word with signs and wonders and miracles. Hallelujah! Awesome!

But the fulfillment of that prophecy depends on your cooperation, doesn't it? God is not going to force you to go get a passport and otherwise prepare yourself for this prophetic calling. He's not going to supernaturally deliver a passport to your mailbox, either. You have to go apply for it like everyone else. He might expedite its processing, but you still have to apply. God will do His part if you do your part. The prophecy may never come to pass if you don't do your part, but that doesn't mean the word was erroneous. When you receive a prophetic word that you have judged to be true, be sure to ask the Lord what you need to do to prepare yourself to receive that promise. Also consider timing. God's timing is important. If we get ahead of God, we can make a mess.

Dangerous Directional Prophecies

Some prophecies are more than presumptuous—they are downright dangerous. Directional prophecies can be an answer to prayer—but they can also be an open door for the enemy to steal, kill and destroy your life. This is another reason why judging prophecy is so critical, no matter what vessel is prophesying.

Consider the story of Mary, who nearly died after following an erroneous directional prophecy:

> "I was told not to get a hysterectomy that had been scheduled because God wanted to heal me and give me children. One prophet told me he saw me dancing with children on the farm. I cancelled the surgery and suffered two more years until I finally had to have it done.
>
> "Thing is, by the time I had the surgery the endometriosis had invaded my bowels and ended up creating a complete blockage from which I almost died—not to mention having to undergo two more

major surgeries. I ended up having three surgeries in eight months.

"Were they prophesying their own desires or mine? I definitely had the faith to be healed and got prayed for by everyone including well-known healing ministers. Not getting healed and not having children as prophesied really turned my husband against God for a few years."

Wow! Mary's story illustrates yet another danger of erroneous prophecy gone bad—it can turn people away from Christ or against God. When prophecy becomes a stumbling block to our faith instead of a means of building us up, you have to question the source.

I am not against directional prophecy if the Lord wants to give it. I believe it can be a great comfort to have understanding. Sometimes we are struggling through something and we can't see the forest for the trees and can't hear the wind for the hurricane. But I caution against applying any directional prophetic word before thoroughly trying it. God expects blind faith in Him, but not blind faith in a prophetic word that you haven't judged. The most well intentioned accurate prophet can miss it. Although I appreciate directional prophecy, I weigh it carefully against the whole counsel of the Word before taking action. When it's true, it also bears witness with my spirit even if my mind goes tilt.

Many people get prophecies about launching into ministry. Some of those prophetic words are must tapping into the idolatry in someone's heart, but some are authentic calls of God. A brother named Gabe told me he received a prophecy three years ago that God wanted to use him in ministry—specifically that God would use him to plant a church.

> "It was not only one prophet that gave me that same word—a number of prophets told me that. For three years the Lord started to use me in different ways. Today I can see His plan in my life. It is just awesome how the Lord blesses us in this ministry. From the first day of the birth of our church, the Lord's grace was with us. We got a church, a beautiful chapel with a thatch roof and chairs. We didn't have to pay anything. God honors obedience. All the glory belongs to Him."

Amen. I share this prophecy and others with you because I want you to be encouraged that there is an abundance of true prophetic words being released in the Body of Christ. We need to be able to receive the true words and throw out the bad ones. But I don't want you to throw out the baby with the bath water, so to speak, so I asked those who follow my ministry to share bona fide prophecies to balance out the questionable ones I also share in this book.

CHAPTER 9

DOES THE PROPHECY PRODUCE FREEDOM?

Now the Lord is that Spirit, and where the Spirit
of the Lord is, there is freedom.

— 2 Corinthians 3:17 (NIV)

It's so important to be a student of the Word. The issue of judging prophecy would not be so mystical for so many if there was a deeper understanding of Christ. It was Jesus who said, "If ye continue in my word, then are ye my disciples indeed; And you shall know the truth, and the truth shall make you free" (John 8:31-32).

The truth always sets us free. Jesus is the Truth. He is the One who hung on a tree to pay the price for our sins and give us eternal life. And it is for freedom that Christ has set us free (Galatians 5:1). If Christ died to liberate us, then the doctrines of Christ—which offer God's thoughts toward us and God's instruction for living—must also be liberating. And so must true prophetic words. If it's truth, it will set us free. If something puts you in bondage, places a heavy burden on your shoulders for which there is no grace, or otherwise oppresses you, it's not from God. Let's look at a few Scriptures that bear this out.

> For as many as are led by the Spirit of God, they are the sons of God. For ye have not received the spirit of bondage again to fear; but ye have received the Spirit of adoption, whereby we cry, Abba, Father.
>
> — Romans 8:14-15

> Take my yoke upon you, and learn of me; for I am meek and lowly in heart: and ye shall find rest unto your souls. For my yoke is easy, and my burden is light.
>
> — Matthew 11:29-30

> And that because of false brethren unawares brought in, who came in privily to spy out our liberty which we have in Christ Jesus, that they might bring us into bondage...
>
> — Galatians 2:4

> Stand fast therefore in the liberty
> wherewith Christ hath made us free, and
> be not entangled again with the yoke of
> bondage.
>
> *— Galatians 5:1*

What truth can we gather from these Scriptures? God's Word won't produce bondage in our lives. His yoke is not oppressive. When the Lord speaks, He gives us the grace to walk in His Word. A prophetic word shouldn't bind you up or press you down. Even if it offers correction or a warning, it should also provide the way of escape. God is not a God of doom and gloom, but of hope and help.

> For I know the thoughts that I
> think toward you, saith the Lord,
> thoughts of peace, and not of evil,
> to give you an expected end.
>
> *— Jeremiah 29:11*

If His thoughts toward us are of peace and not of evil, wouldn't His prophetic words be, too? Yet false brethren, Paul warned, will work to bring you into bondage. Remember, where the Spirit of the Lord is there is freedom. So if the prophetic word came from the Spirit of the Lord, then it will produce freedom in your life—or it will show the way to freedom.

Can I Buy A Prophetic Word, Please?

Oh, and while we are on the topic of free let me address something else that's unscriptural: charging people for personal prophecy. I've seen far too much of this in $1,000 prayer lines over the years. But with the Internet the merchandising trend has exploded. False prophets are actually taking out Google search engine marketing ads to offer services like "daily prophetic words."

Some of these Internet prophets are subtle. They guise their merchandising schemes by using a tactic that museums often employ: collecting a "suggested offering" at the door. Such tactics lower prophetic ministry to the level of palm-reading, crystal ball-gazing psychics. The only difference is, most psychics charge $5. False prophets charge much, much more.

Jesus said, "freely ye have received, freely give" (Matthew 10:8). Oh sure, I can hear the religious prophets now citing that whole Scripture. So let's address that. Jesus said, "Heal the sick, cleanse the lepers, raise the dead, cast out devils: freely ye have received, freely give."

Granted, Jesus did not specifically mention prophetic words in that Scripture. But we live by the Spirit and not by the letter. In other words, the spirit of what Jesus is saying is this: Don't charge money to exercise your spiritual gifts. Let's be clear: I'm certainly NOT saying that you can't charge for books, CDs, conferences, etc. I'm not saying that you can't receive offerings if someone wants to bless you. I am saying that you should NOT hang a shingle on your web site offering to e-mail people who are confused and hurting with a prophetic word. Did you see Jesus doing this?

He is our prototype Prophet. Prophets are supposed to equip people to discern the voice of God, not charge them to go into a prayer closet and manufacture a prophetic word that probably didn't come from heaven.

What's next? Prophetic auctions that sell a prophetic utterance to the highest bidder? Don't be fooled. You can hear from God for yourself. You don't need a prophet to speak into your life. You need a prophet to equip you to hear from God and judge what you hear. That's what this book is all about.

Freedom From Doubt

Sometimes we step out in faith and we don't see what we expected. In fact, sometimes the exact opposite of what our faith expected occurs. When this happens, it's easy enough to question whether or not you missed God. This is Shaneen's story. But thank God a prophetic word came that brought her liberty.

> "Recently I moved to Florida. Before the move it looked liked things were not lining up and I began to question if I really heard God. But after I moved I received a prophecy. The prophet said, 'You've been praying and praying. God is coming in like a mighty rushing wind and He is going to part the red sea. You're going over on dry land. And you will not sink anymore.' The prophet said so much more but that word helped me a lot. Some people thought I was crazy for moving and I started to

question God. But everything shortly fell right into place and what was prophesied came to pass quickly."

Thank God. Where the Spirit of the Lord is there is liberty—even if it doesn't look like liberty round and about you. This prophetic word comforted Shaneen and set her free from her doubts about whether or not she had heard from God. That is what I call liberating!

CHAPTER 10

DOES THE PROPHECY
SEEK TO CONTROL?

You put up with it when someone enslaves you, takes everything
you have, takes advantage of you, takes control of everything, and
slaps you in the face.

– 2 Corinthians 11:20 (NLT)

We have a free will. God doesn't try to control us. Yet
some people use prophecy as a tool to manipulate and
control. These prophets and prophetic people have the
wrong motive. It may be financial gain, a need to draw
people to themselves for service of some sort, or
another hidden agenda. Controlling prophets may be
fleshly prophets—or they may have a spirit of control
operating in their lives.

Either way, if a prophecy makes you feel forced,
abused, or otherwise pushed to go in a direction you
don't feel right about, it should raise a red flag in your
spirit. God has given us a free will and He will never
usurp it. He may work to persuade us or draw us, but

He does it in a spirit of love rather than a spirit of control. God is love.

Gina wrote me a message that offers some practical experience in this area:

> "God's ways are not our ways. We may hear a prophecy and not fully understand it's meaning at the time. I had things told to me when I was 12 years old that have just recently come to pass.

> "Anything that is spoken to manipulate you or control you is a spirit of witchcraft. I have seen lives really messed up because some one told them to marry a certain person. If God has someone for you, He will lead both of you in that direction by His Spirit. Be careful who you let speak words of prophecy, lay hands on you or pray for you. There are so many abuses of prophecy.

> "You must know the Spirit of God and discern by the Holy Spirit and the Word of God. The Bible will confirm prophecy in Scripture."

Amen, Gina!

Jezebel's Controlling Prophets

Although there is a difference between the spirit of control and the spirit of Jezebel (Jezebel is so much more than control alone) Jezebel often manifests with control. When you hear prophetic judgments and curses that are clearly not coming from the heart of God, you may be dealing with one of Jezebel's modern day prophets. Just like Queen Jezebel released fearful death threats in the Old Testament, New Testament prophets consumed with the spirit of Jezebel continue to release fearful death threats in the form of judgments and curses.

Here's how it works: The prophets of Jezebel prophesy smooth flattering words to manipulate and control. If that doesn't work, they transition into warfare mode and prophesy fearful sayings to control you.

Some of Jezebel's playgrounds are insecurities, rejection and hidden fears. Since everybody is insecure about something, no one is immune to Jezebel. Jezebel probes your soul to discover your insecurities and hidden fears so she can exploit them later.

Flattery works well on folks who have insecurities and hidden fears or rejection. Jezebel can smooth talk them. Jezebel can tell them how great a singer they are or how powerful a preacher they are. Whether it's true or not, they'll receive it because they want to. It makes them feel better about their insecure selves. Then Jezebel can manipulate and tap into their pride. (We all have pride, too.) Jezebel will tell them how they should be elevated to a more visible position in the ministry. Jezebel will tell them how their gift should be making more room for them.

What Are You Insecure About?

Suffice it to say Jezebel will seek to control you by petting insecurities and alleviating your hidden fears. What are you insecure about? What are you afraid of? Our confidence should be in Christ in us. He hasn't given us a spirit of fear, but of power, love and a sound mind (2 Timothy 1:7).

Unfortunately, it seems the spirit of Jezebel has already hijacked some segments of the prophetic ministry. Like a terrorist who extorts, swindles or coerces a pilot at gunpoint, the Jezebel spirit is kidnapping prophets who have unresolved character issues, bitterness, hurts and wounds and using them for sinister purposes.

I've said it before and I'll keep saying it. I don't believe false prophets start out as false prophets. I believe they go astray somewhere on the road to Christ-likeness. We need prophets and intercessors that hear the Spirit accurately and can stand with integrity in the ministries to which they've been called. I believe there are more who are standing in integrity than who aren't. We may not know who they are. But we must judge all prophecy because many false prophets have gone out into the world—and the spirit of Jezebel is also running loose. Any prophecy that seeks to control you should be dismissed.

CHAPTER 11

DOES THE PROPHECY BREED FEAR?

For God hath not given us the spirit of fear; but of power, and of love, and of a sound mind.

— 2 Timothy 1:7

There's only one type of fear a prophecy should breed: reverential fear and awe of the Lord our God. I am going to say that again in a different way because it's important as we establish the foundation for this chapter. Prophetic words should cause a certain reverential fear of God—God Almighty is speaking directly to us!—but prophecy should not cause us to be frightened about what is going to happen.

God did not give us a spirit of fear, but of power, love and a sound mind (2 Timothy 1:7). If God did not give us a spirit of fear—and He didn't—then God doesn't want us to be fearful. That sounds as simple as "Jesus loves me. This I know, for the Bible tells me so." But there is power in the fundamentals. If you can remember this truth, you'll save yourself and others a lot of anxiety. God does not want us to be scared. That's why His Word tells us over and over and over again to "fear not."

Two Types of Fear

The fear of the Lord produces good fruit. It's the beginning of wisdom and understanding (Psalm 111:10). It leads to life, rest, peace and contentment (Proverbs 19:23). It is the fountain of life (Proverbs 14:27). It offers security and safety (Proverbs 14:26). The list goes on and on.

By contrast, the spirit of fear produces rotten fruit. Fear can cause many unpleasant actions and manifestations. Fear can cause sleep disturbances, tightness in your chest, nightmares, fatigue, helplessness, depression, guilt, poor appetite, and a host of other symptoms. In short, fear hath torment. The medical world lists 366 causes of fear. I'd like to add one: scary false prophecies.

If the prophetic word comes from God, even if He's warning us about something unpleasant coming down the line, it's not going to breed sheer terror in our hearts. Think of Noah. God told Him that He was going to bring a flood on the earth and gave Him instructions to build the ark. We don't see Noah having an anxiety attack, biting his nails or staying awake all night fretting. God warned Him of impending danger, but He also equipped Him for victory. So, yes, a prophetic word can warn you of something unpleasant around the corner—but it will also give you the way of escape so that you don't have to be fearful. As long as we follow God, He will deliver us into victory through every circumstance. We don't have to be afraid. Noah had a reverential fear of the Lord. That's what we need to maintain.

So many times fear deals with the unknown. We fear because we don't know what's going to happen. Many times I think well-intentioned prophets miss it by moving on to the next person in the prayer line before God is finished speaking. I experienced this personally once. A true prophet spoke over me that I was about to experience a season of trials; that it was going to be lengthy and difficult. The prophetic word was true, but it was partial. And because it was partial, it caused plenty of anxiety. I didn't know what was about to happen. I could only imagine. And my imagination was running wild. The prophet left off the edifying portion of the prophetic word. The part about how the trials were going to bring me to a new land of opportunity. Instead of being encouraged, I left the prayer line wondering what in the world was about to happen that was going to "cause me to second guess myself and my ministry."

How Erroneous Prophecy Brings Fear

I started to title this section "How False Prophecy Breeds Fear." Then I changed it because true prophets who miss it can release words that breed fear as well. I had someone prophesy over me once that my "destiny is not settled."

Well, that's more than a little disturbing to say the least. The Bible has plenty to say about our destiny in Christ. It made no sense to me—and in fact it disturbed my spirit and caused me to get a little anxious—that my destiny would be unsettled. After praying about it, I realized I needed to stick with the written Word of God. My destiny is settled in Christ. I dismissed the prophetic word, even though it came from someone I respected. God did not say that.

Please remember this: When it comes to prophetic words, don't receive something you don't bear witness to—or something that causes fear—just because it came from someone in authority. Scripture is the ultimate authority we submit our lives to. If the prophecy contradicts Scripture, it's not from God. I don't care how anointed the prophet is. If he is spewing fearful prophetic utterances, don't submit to those words. Too often people are ostracized in churches, or labeled as deceived, because they question what comes from the pulpit. We have a right to question, in the right spirit, what is being preached or prophesied. In fact, we have a responsibility to ourselves to do so. If we don't, we're bound to fall into the end-time deception that will lead to the great falling away (2 Thessalonians 2:3).

False Prophets Manipulate with Fear

So let's take a look at the other side of the coin: false prophets, or people who make prophetic announcements with the intent to manipulate and control using fear. There's a strong example in Nehemiah. Let's listen in to how Nehemiah handled the false prophetic missives that were launched against him. As you do, keep in mind that these words were released to get him to step out of the will of God.

Let me set the stage. Nehemiah's enemies heard that he had built the wall and there was no breach left in it. Nehemiah and his faithful crew were forging ahead to set up the doors in the gates. Two of Nehemiah's enemies, Sanballat and Geshem, wanted to meet with in a nearby village—with the intent of doing him harm. Nehemiah discerned their motives and declined their invitation. They tried this four times. Each time Nehemiah said no.

Next, Nehemiah's enemies made up a false report about him. They used a fearful tactic to get Nehemiah to stop the work and come meet with them. That didn't work either. Nehemiah wasn't buying it. The enemy's next move to was to send in a hired false prophet. Let's listen in:

> Afterward I came unto the house of Shemaiah the son of Delaiah the son of Mehetabeel, who was shut up; and he said, Let us meet together in the house of God, within the temple, and let us shut the doors of the temple: for they will come to slay thee; yea, in the night will they come to slay thee.
>
> And I said, Should such a man as I flee? and who is there, that, being as I am, would go into the temple to save his life? I will not go in.
>
> And, lo, I perceived that God had not sent him; but that he pronounced this

prophecy against me: for Tobiah and Sanballat had hired him.

Therefore was he hired, that I should be afraid, and do so, and sin, and that they might have matter for an evil report, that they might reproach me.

– Nehemiah 6:10-13

Wow. In a nutshell, the enemy hired a false prophet to try to scare Nehemiah out of God's will. And that's the enemy's plan with false prophecy: to get you out of God's perfect will. Sometimes he does it with greed seeds. Other times he does it with fear seeds. Still other times he does it with pride seeds or some other lie. This is another reason why it's so vital to judge prophecy. The devil can even use a well-meaning true prophet's erroneous utterance to wreak havoc in your life. Do you want to build your life on lies from the enemy? Or do you want to build your life on the truth from Jesus? I already know your answer.

Whether the prophecy causes you to fear, or whether you discern that it's supposed to cause you to fear—reject it! Reject it immediately. Bind those words spoken over your life—in the name of Jesus. Do not submit yourself to fear in any size, shape or color. Do not bow to control or manipulation in any flavor. You don't have to confront the prophet who released the word. But don't receive it, don't repeat it and don't think about it. Instead, find a Scripture that counters what was spoken and confess it over your life.

Scaring Baby Christians

One precious woman named Stephanie wrote to tell me her story. I am running it in its entirety as she offered it. As you read this, ask the Holy Spirit to help you see what's wrong with this picture.

> "My husband and I had only been saved a few months and filled with the Spirit. We were invited to a home prayer meeting and decided to go. At the end of the meeting, before we left, a lady prophesied to us that Satan was going to try and kill us on the way home, but that God and His mighty power would stop it.

> We were so in fear at this word. What was going to happen? Would we be injured but not killed? How had we opened the door to this? It was the longest 20-minute drive we have ever experienced. Such fear was over us and we were just waiting for a car to slam into us or something tragic to happen. We arrived home but we were so upset. We never went back to that prayer group."

Your first instinct might be to think, "Well, what was wrong with that? She was warning them of the attack, but assured them God would stop the attack." There are a couple of things wrong with this "prophecy." First, this woman was operating in presumption. Did she take the time to pray and ask God if she was supposed to release that word? (I highly doubt it, seeing as it didn't originate from God in the first place.) When you receive a word from the Lord that may disturb someone, you shouldn't automatically release it. Maybe you are just supposed to pray. Always consider this: How would you feel if someone said that to you? More importantly, ask God if He wants you to say it.

Second, if this woman really was hearing from the Lord about some sort of attack against these baby Christians, she could have handled it with wisdom. Instead of terrorizing the poor couple, she could have simply suggested the group pray for them as they went. The prayer group could have prayed for God's angels to surround them, could have pled the blood of Jesus over them, and so on. If the woman was that convinced she heard from God, she could have interceded until she was sure they had gotten home. Putting such fear in them could have actually caused them to make a dangerous mistake while driving.

This irresponsible woman scared the daylights out of these baby Christians. Nothing even resembling the prophetic word came to pass. All it did was breed fear and anxiety. Luckily, Stephanie and her husband did not dismiss the existence of true prophetic ministry based on this experience. Unfortunately, many others have. And who could blame them? With so much fear, manipulation and control lacing prophetic words, sometimes it takes discernment, maturity and faith to wade through the mire. Baby Christians don't always have that discernment and maturity.

True Prophetic Erases Fear

While false prophecy can breed fear, true prophecy can do just the opposite: deliver from fear. Terri tells me about a prophecy that gave her the courage to undergo an operation that forever changed her life for the better. I'll let her tell the story in her own words:

> "In 1987, I responded to an altar call given by a visiting minister from Africa. When he placed his hand on my head and spoke, the words really bore witness with my spirit. He said, 'I will take the bashfulness out of your mouth. I will use you in ways that you never thought possible and I will give you strength.' This told me that something was going to give. I already had the 'want' in me to have this surgery. However, I did not feel courageous, like I was ready yet. This was the icing on the cake that got me to that point. He brought healing and set me free. God was in this. He led me to talk to the right agencies and people. Things really started happening after that. Soon, a Christian hospital called. It was set up for me to come have extensive testing and then, neurosurgery. The surgery was success. I am seizure-free. Praise God!"

Praise God is right! All healings aren't like the miracles we see in the Bible. Joyce Meyer had a mastectomy after she was diagnosed with breast cancer, for example. God gave us doctors. The prophecy to Terri helped her overcome a fear and free herself from seizures forever. The prophecy edified and comforted her. That's part and parcel of prophecy.

CHAPTER 12

DOES THE PROPHECY PRODUCE STABILITY?

...It is impossible for God to lie, we might have strong consolation, who have fled for refuge to lay hold of the hope set before us. This hope we have as an anchor of the soul, both sure and steadfast...

– Hebrews 6:18-19

God is not unstable. His Word is not unstable. His ways are not unstable. Therefore, anything that proceeds from the mouth of God should not produce instability in you. True prophetic words will make you more stable, offering solid ground for you to build on as you continue toward your destiny in Christ. Erroneous or false prophecy has the opposite effect: it produces instability.

Let's look at the definitions of "stable" and "instable" in light of Scripture. This exercise will help build in you the truth to recognize prophetic words that could lead you into instability and out of God's best life for you.

Scripturally Sound

Merriam-Webster defines stable as "firmly established, fixed, steadfast; not changing or fluctuating: unvarying; permanent, enduring." That reminds me of what Paul told the church at Colosse: "So then, just as you have received Christ Jesus as Lord, continue to live in him, rooted and built up in him, strengthened in the faith as you were taught, and overflowing with thankfulness" (Colossians 2:7-8 NIV). Paul prayed that we would be, "rooted and established in love" (Ephesians 3:18). This is a picture of stability in Christ. This is what we are called to.

Another definition of stable is "steady in purpose: firm in resolution." That reminds me of Paul's proclamation: "Brethren, I count not myself to have apprehended: but this one thing I do, forgetting those things which are behind, and reaching forth unto those things which are before, I press toward the mark for the prize of the high calling of God in Christ Jesus" (Philippians 3:13-14). Paul was steady in purpose. At the end of his life, he was able to say, "I have fought a good fight, I have finished my course, I have kept the faith" (2 Timothy 4:7).

That's stable. That's what prophetic words should help establish in your life: stability. Of course, it's up to you to do your part to walk in stability by renewing your mind with the Word and walking in the principles of the Spirit. But prophetic words shouldn't be a stumbling block on your path. They should edify, comfort and exhort you as you continue walking steadfast in the faith, steady in purpose, intent on finishing your course for the glory of God.

Unstable Prophecies

The opposite of stable is unstable. To be unstable is to be "not stable: not firm or fixed: not constant; not steady in action or movement; wavering in purpose or intent; lacking steadiness: apt to move, sway or fall; characterized by lack of emotional control."

So let's look at instability from a Scriptural perspective. First of all, we know that the Bible says a double-minded man is unstable in all his ways (James 1:8). A double-minded man isn't walking by faith. He's like a wave of the sea driven with the wind and tossed. The true prophetic word should help stabilize believers who, for whatever reason, aren't stable or who are wavering in some area of their lives.

> And he gave some, apostles; and some, prophets; and some, evangelists; and some, pastors and teachers; For the perfecting of the saints, for the work of the ministry, for the edifying of the body of Christ: Till we all come in the unity of the faith, and of the knowledge of the Son of God, unto a perfect man, unto the measure of the stature of the fulness of Christ:

That we henceforth be no more children, tossed to and fro, and carried about with every wind of doctrine, by the sleight of men, and cunning craftiness, whereby they lie in wait to deceive; But speaking the truth in love, may grow up into him in all things, which is the head, even Christ: From whom the whole body fitly joined together and compacted by that which every joint supplieth, according to the effectual working in the measure of every part, maketh increase of the body unto the edifying of itself in love.

– Ephesians 4:11-16

If true prophets are doing their job—and in some cases I should say if true prophets are allowed to do their job—I believe there would be far fewer double-minded, unstable Christians. The true prophetic brings stability and maturity. False prophets, on the other hand, prey on the emotionally unstable to fulfill their own evil purposes. Emotionally unstable people are more likely to buy into the hype machine. Rather than patiently believing God for the breakthrough, for example, they'll literally buy into manipulative prophecies that leave their pocketbooks empty and their souls jaded. Too many have blamed God for not doing what He never said He'd do. The prophet spoke for God without permission.

Peter was talking about false prophets when he said: "Having eyes full of adultery, and that cannot cease from sin; beguiling unstable souls: an heart they have exercised with covetous practices; cursed children" (2 Peter 2:14). False prophets prey on the unstable. If you see instability in your life, shore up your soul with the Word of God so you will not fall into this error.

You Can Hear God

Prophetic ministry can be abused. Sometimes, abusive prophetic ministry produces unstable Christians who are dependent more on the prophet than on the Prophet (Jesus). I have heard far too many stories of Christians who go to prophets for confirmation about decisions they are trying to make.

I'm not saying it's wrong, in theory, to seek confirmation from a more mature believer. I would recommend it, especially to people who are younger in the Lord. I'm warning you about being too dependent on a prophet when God has equipped you to be led by His Spirit. There's a balance in all things, right? Yes, if you believe the prophets you shall prosper (2 Chronicles 20:20). But prophets who are toeing the party line—that is, prophets who are more loyal to a church, an apostle, or something else other than God—could possibly tell you what they think is best for the party line rather than what is God's best for you. These prophets may not consciously know that they are leading you astray. They may just have a bent toward believing whatever benefits the local church is God's will for you. But that's not always so.

I fell into this trap once. I felt led of God to go to a foreign nation in need of humanitarian help, but I wasn't sure about the timing. I didn't want to disappoint the evangelist who invited me—and I really did want to go. But the timing was horrendous. It would have thrown a major kink in several areas of my life—interrupting events to which I had already committed. I didn't really have peace about going on that specific flight, though I did believe I was being called to go there. Because I was concerned about disappointing the evangelist, I sought the confirmation of a prophet in the church I was attending at the time. I'm being completely transparent here. I thought the prophet would tell me not to go—and that would make it easier to tell the eager evangelist "no." I figured would simply go on another trip at a later date.

Well, to my surprise, the prophet told me, "I saw you in Haiti. Go and let your joint supply." Oddly enough, when she said that I knew I wasn't supposed to go. It didn't bear witness with my spirit at all. So, in a way, it was confirmation. Just not the kind I expected. God worked my foolish mistake together for good. He showed me what to do. As it turned out, this evangelist was merely using me for my media gifts anyway. The evangelist's motive was questionable. Remember, the Bible says, "For as many as are led by the Spirit of God, they are the sons of God" (Romans 8:14). It doesn't say, "For as many as are led by the prophets of God, they are the sons of God."

True maturity in Christ is being able to hear from the Holy Spirit yourself. There's nothing wrong with getting others to judge what you've heard. But you need to be careful about with whom you share what the Lord has put on your heart. Well-meaning people can talk you out of God's will and into their will without even realizing what they are doing. Remember, Jesus said, "My sheep hear my voice, and I know them, and they follow me" (John 10:27). Follow Jesus. He'll never steer you wrong.

Becky's Confirmation

Last year Becky received prophecy that she was going to be able to share her testimony with more people, which was a confirmation of her prayers. The prophetic word rang true in her spirit so she took immediate action.

> "I knew that I was to write my testimony down after receiving the prophecy. From writing and sending it to various people as I was led, I was then asked to give it. In giving it, me and another friend met a wonderful couple who leased a building that was to used for ministry. This friend and I knew based on a prophetic word and how God was leading that we were to open a prayer ministry—inner healing, Healing Rooms and intercessory prayer. The prayer room has now been open for approximately eight months! It is amazing how God put this all together."

Praise God! Some people wait years to see the manifestation of a true prophetic word in their lives. So don't get discouraged if it seems to be taking a while to see a prophetic word you deem to be true come to pass. Hold on to what the Spirit of God said if you believe the Spirit of God said it. And do like Becky did—take whatever action you can as you wait for God to fulfill the word. Prepare yourself to receive the fulfillment.

Unexpected Prophecies

Sometimes prophecies don't bear witness at all. These prophecies don't violate the principles of Scripture, but they just don't seem to line up with what you have planned for your life. That doesn't mean it's not God. Keep an open mind with prophecy. If the prophecy doesn't bear witness with your spirit, but it's not anything that violates Scripture, breeds fear, causes confusion, or some other bad fruit, then put it on the shelf. It could be for a good many years down the road. The prophecy will serve as a confirmation later in your life. That was the case with Andrea. Let's listen in to her experience:

> "I was given a prophetic word that I had the qualities necessary to be working with children. I hadn't thought of that being the field I should work in, but I took a job working with children and I must say it's been one of the most rewarding experiences of my life. As a matter of fact, I changed my field of study to go into early childhood education."

Likewise, Bev was given a prophecy in 1988 that made no sense to her at all—and it was nearly three pages long. Let's see how she handled it—and what the outcome was.

"I put the prophecy away and forgot about it. One day in 2003 the Lord reminded me of it. I was amazed as I read it to see that it described the life I had just lived and I was right where the prophecy said I would be. 2003 was the year God began to show me that I was a prophet. I have to say I wasn't happy about it. I was scared witless. So the moral to my little story is: don't throw away a prophecy just because it doesn't make sense at the moment you get it. Hold on to it. Tuck it away in an old diary and wait for the Lord's perfect timing."

Indeed. You can always 'put the prophecy on the shelf.' So long as it doesn't send up a red flag in your spirit, violate Scripture, or seek to control or manipulate you, you can put it on the shelf. If you see abundant bad fruit surrounding the prophetic word, throw it out.

PART 3

THE CLARITY TESTS

Give me understanding, and I shall keep thy law; yea, I shall observe it with my whole heart.

– Psalm 119:34

Clarity. That's what we all want from God, right? Clear direction for our lives? We don't want to live a life shrouded in mystery. We want to be wise; understanding the will of the Lord. The written Word of God offers us plenty of direction, but sometimes we need the Spirit of God to speak to our hearts—and sometimes He speaks through prophets—with specific instructions about what to do next.

Let's face it. What college to attend, what job to take, which house to buy, whom to marry, and other major life decisions—and even smaller ones—aren't outlined in the Bible. Yet, we still want to be in God's perfect will. So what should we do? We should acknowledge Him in all our ways and trust Him to direct our paths like His Word says (Proverbs 3:6). We acknowledge Him by studying His Word on a topic, praying about it, and waiting on His direction.

Think about it for a minute. Why would a loving God who promises to direct our paths when we acknowledge Him cloak His direction in mystery? Sure, He may only give us a tiny part of the direction, but the part He gives will be clear. Otherwise, how can He expect us to obey? It would be unjust for God to expect us to obey a direction that could have several very different meanings—or that is so obscure no one can make sense of it.

God is not unjust. Again, He may give us an ounce of direction so that we will be inspired to seek His face for the next ounce. But ultimately He's not trying to hide the truth from us. God may hide the truth about our destinies from the devil to protect us, but when the time comes for us to gain understanding about where to go and what to do next, God is not going to hide that truth from us. What purpose would that serve but to delay His will?

The Bible says those who are led by the Spirit of God are the sons of God (Romans 8:14). How can the Spirit of God lead us if we don't have clarity on what He's saying. David said, "Give me understanding, and I shall keep thy law; yea, I shall observe it with my whole heart" (Psalm 119:34).

The Spirit of God is more than capable of making Himself clear. What benefit does He get by giving us a prayer answer or prophecy that leaves us confused in the middle of a major life decision? God is love and every single solitary action He takes is motivated by His love for us. If we seek the truth, we will find it. We may have to press in a little harder. We may need to repent of some things. But if we seek Him, we will find Him—and we will come to know His will.

I've had some religious types persecute me for saying these things. They tell me the Bible can't be understood, and all prophecy is ambiguous. If that's the truth, we shouldn't bother to read the Bible and we should ban prophetic ministry from the Church right now because it's all a waste of time at best and distracts us from soul-winning at worst. Yes, in the Old Testament there are examples of dark sayings and in the New Testament Jesus often spoke in parables. But even in the Old Testament there are abundant examples of prophets giving crystal clear instructions. And Jesus explained His parables to His true disciples when they inquired.

When Isaiah prophesied to Hezekiah that he would live seven more years, was it clear? (2 Kings 18:5). Or did Hezekiah sit and wonder how much longer he would live? When Elijah prophesied that it would not rain but according to his word, was it clear? (1 Kings 17:1) Or did the people wonder what he meant? What about the time Elijah prophesied to the woman that her meal and oil would not run out until the Lord sent rain on the earth (1 Kings 17:14)? Did the woman wonder if he meant her spiritual oil or her natural oil? Of course not. The Spirit of God was clear. I'm not saying you can't expound on a prophetic word by supplementing what the Lord said with the Word of God to bring another level of understanding. I'm saying that the Holy Spirit can make Himself clear. He wants us to get understanding. He's not talking to hear Himself talk or to impress the other members of the Trinity with His riddling skills. He's trying to lead us into all truth.

Oh, but Jesus spoke in parables. He wasn't prophesying in parables. He was teaching in parables in order that Scripture might be fulfilled (Matthew 13:35). And He offered a good reason why.

> And he said unto them, Unto you it is given to know the mystery of the kingdom of God: but unto them that are without, all these things are done in parables: That seeing they may see, and not perceive; and hearing they may hear, and not understand; lest at any time they should be converted, and their sins should be forgiven them.
>
> —Mark 4:11-12

We are already converted. Our sins are already forgiven. We are kings and priests in His Kingdom. He's not trying to hide the truth from us. Actually, Jesus was frustrated with His disciples that they didn't understand—and they weren't even filled with the Holy Ghost yet. He would speak to the crowds in parables, then His disciples would come to Him asking what He meant. Jesus' response, "Are ye also yet without understanding?" (Matthew 15:16) and "Know ye not this parable? How then will ye know all parables?" (Mark 4:13).

Again, Jesus wasn't typically prophesying in parables. And when He taught in parables and His disciples didn't understand it, He took the time to explain it to them when they asked Him. When Jesus spoke in parables, even the hard-hearted religious leaders sometimes understood that He was talking about them (Matthew 21:45).

The bottom line: The Apostle Paul warns us not to be unwise, but to understand what the will of the Lord is (Ephesians 5:17). Why would the Holy Spirit tell us to be sure to understand what His will us, and then offer a muddy prophetic word that leaves us running in confused circles? I submit to you that He wouldn't. That's not His style.

I'm sure I've overemphasized my point here. But it's such an important one that I wanted to hammer it in. As you read these next few chapters, I pray that God will give you understanding in this so that you can judge prophetic words accurately.

CHAPTER 13

IS THE PROPHECY
AMBIGUOUS?

*Now the Spirit speaketh expressly, that in the latter
times some shall depart from the faith, giving heed to
seducing spirits, and doctrines of devils.*

— 1 Timothy 4:1

Have you ever received a prophetic word that was
more than a little ambiguous? Ambiguous means
"capable of being understood in two or more possible
senses or ways." In other words, there's a lot of grey
area in there. You could take it to mean this, that or
something else. It's just not clear what the Spirit of
God meant. Or did the Spirit of God really even say
that?

It's possible that it wasn't God at all. The Bible says
that the Holy Spirit speaks expressly, clearly, explicitly,
and distinctly, depending on which translation of 1
Timothy 4:1 you read. Whatever version you prefer,
one thing is certain: there's no ambiguity.

Now, I am not implying that we always understand the full meaning of a prophetic word any more than we understand the full meaning of Scripture. There can be layers of revelation in a prophetic word. We could also be spiritually dull and just not get it. What I'm trying to point out to you is this: God is not trying to be mysterious. Yes, He may give you a word or phrase so that you'll seek Him for the whole truth. But ultimately God is not trying to hide the truth from you or play word games. That doesn't serve His purposes.

Ambiguity in Action

Let me give you a broad example of an ambiguous prophecy, then we'll drive it home to our personal lives. Joseph Smith is the founder of the Church of Jesus Christ of Latter-day Saints, also known as the Mormon Church. In the Doctrines & Covenants, a Mormon supplement to the Bible, Smith wrote:

> "I was once praying very earnestly to know the time of the coming of the Son of Man, when I heard a voice repeat the following:

> 'Joseph, my son, if thou livest until thou art eighty-five years old, thou shalt see the face of the Son of Man; therefore let this suffice, and trouble me no more on this matter.'

I was left thus, without being able to decide whether this coming referred to the beginning of the millennium or to some previous appearing, or whether I should die and thus see his face. I believe the coming of the Son of Man will not be any sooner than that time."

First of all, you have to wonder what voice Smith was listening to. There are many voices out there in the spirit realm. Second, Smith would have been 85 in 1890—if he hadn't been murdered by a mob first. But the larger point is the ambiguity of the prophecy. You could interpret it to mean that Jesus would return in the year 1890. Clearly, that didn't happen. But you could also interpret it that 1890 would pass without the Lord's return. That, of course, is true.

21st Century Ambiguity

Have you ever received an ambiguous prophecy? A synonym of ambiguous is obscure. Obscure means "shrouded in or hidden by darkness; not clearly seen or easily distinguished; not readily understood or clearly expressed; mysterious." We are in the Kingdom of Light. Why would God utter something shrouded in darkness? He generally wouldn't. The Holy Spirit speaks clearly in these times. Consider these Scriptures:

I have told you these things in parables (veiled language, allegories, dark sayings); the hour is now coming when I shall no longer speak to you in figures of speech, but I shall tell you about the Father in plain words and openly (without reserve) (John 16:25 AMP).

And again, "The entrance of thy words giveth light; it giveth understanding unto the simple" (Psalm 119:130).

For the Lord giveth wisdom: out of his mouth cometh knowledge and understanding (Proverbs 2:6)

Yet in the church I had rather speak five words with my understanding, that by my voice I might teach others also, than ten thousand words in an unknown tongue (1 Corinthians 14:19).

Who also declared unto us your love in the Spirit. For this cause we also, since the day we heard it, do not cease to pray for you, and to desire that ye might be filled with the knowledge of his will in all wisdom and spiritual understanding; That ye might walk worthy of the Lord unto all pleasing, being fruitful in every good work, and increasing in the knowledge of God (Colossians 1:8-10).

Consider what I say; and the Lord give thee understanding in all things (2 Timothy 2:7).

Again and again, we see Scripture that makes it clear that God wants us to be clear on His will. He wants us to understand what He is saying. He wants us to obtain knowledge and wisdom from His words. Although prophecy can certainly be symbolic and we may have to dig below the surface to find the meaning, when we seek the truth we will find the truth. We may have to press in, but God is ultimately going to reveal His meaning so you aren't left bewildered and wandering aimlessly wondering what His will is.

Some false prophets are purposely ambiguous with their feigned prophetic utterances. These are conmen of the cloth, so to speak, offering prophetic words that are so vague that it's difficult to prove them wrong on the merits of the word alone. That's why we have to judge the word from several angles, at times, to discern its validity.

The "If Clause"

Let me take you on a quick bunny trail. Some prophets use what I call the "if clause." They prophesy some grand event that's going to take place, but then put the "if" clause at the end of it. You've heard these prophecies. "If this happens, then God won't do that" or "If this doesn't happen, then God will do this." I'm not saying that prophecy can't be conditional or that you should reject prophecies that contain the "if clause." There are valid examples in the Bible of conditional prophecies (read: Nineveh). I am just concerned that some prophets are using the "if clause" to give themselves a way out of their presumptuous prophecies.

Ridiculously Funny Prophecies

To end on a lighter note, some prophecies are ambiguous but others are simply ridiculous. An apostle sent me a message with something that sounds like it should be an advertisement for Microsoft: "I had a 'prophet' tell me that in order for God to move in my life I had to change my computer operating system to Windows Vista." Even Microsoft admits that Windows Vista was the worst mistake the company ever made in its software development history! And what does your computer operating system have to do with your destiny? Laughable.

A woman named Brenda shared another ridiculous prophecy with me. "A prophet told me that I'm a prophet with the abilities of a physic. He said I could see people's souls and people fear me. He said I'm going to strange places unknown far, far away. That was very odd to me." Odd, indeed. We all know how the Lord feels about psychics. And a prophet of God certainly doesn't need the "abilities of a psychic."

Jason shared with me a ridiculous prophecy he received from a so-called prophet. "The prophet told me God was going to be my genie and give me seven wishes: three for my prophetic anointing, three for my apostolic anointing and one concerning my wife." Um... really?

Lisa got a prophecy assuring her that when she "got rich" God was going to keep her from getting plastic surgery. And Anne tells me about a ridiculous prophecy she received that went something like this: "Your prophetic gifting is so powerful and God trusts you so much with it that your clothes will be afraid to be on my body! I'm not even walking in the office of a prophetess. I'm a deaconess. And I didn't know clothes could be afraid."

Those kind of prophecies remind me of a photo I saw recently of a sign out on the sidewalk that said, "Psychic Fair Cancelled Due to Unforeseen Circumstances." Still, for all the ambiguous prophecy floating around out there, true prophecy is still alive and well. We just have to learn to judge the difference.

CHAPTER 14

DOES THE PROPHECY BRING MAJOR CONFUSION?

The spirits of the prophets are subject to the prophets. For God is not the author of confusion, but of peace, as in all churches of the saints.

— 1 Corinthians 14:32-33

The spirits of the prophets are subject to the prophets. For God is not the author of confusion, but of peace, as in all churches of the saints. Think about that Scripture for a moment. Verse 32 is often cited in prophetic ministry apart from Verse 33. In other words, both verses are sometimes used separately and out of context. But let's put these verses back into context for a moment: The Holy Spirit distinctly connected the need for prophets to use self-control in order to avoid confusion and disorder.

True prophetic ministry should bring peace, not turmoil, to your spirit. God is a God of Peace

(Hebrews 13:20). Jesus is the Prince of Peace. The Holy Spirit is the Spirit of Peace. Even if the prophetic word causes our soul to run a million miles a minute thinking about how, when or why the prophecy will come to pass, a true prophetic word should bring peace—not confusion—to our spirits. Prophecy is spiritually discerned, so even if our souls begin to work overtime trying to make sense of the prophetic word, our spirits will bear witness to true prophecy. Your spirit bears witness through peace.

> And let the peace (soul harmony which comes) from Christ rule (act as umpire continually) in your hearts [deciding and settling with finality all questions that arise in your minds, in that peaceful state] to which as [members of Christ's] one body you were also called [to live].
>
> —Colossians 3:15 (AMP)

Let's compare confusion with peace for a moment so you can get a crystal clear picture of the difference in your spirit. Remember, I'm talking about spiritual peace here. You can have soulish peace and still be out of the will of God. If the prophecy speaks to the idolatry in your heart, your soul may be peaceful because your ears are tickled. But if you search a little deeper, your spirit will not bear witness with an untrue prophetic word. We need to get past this surface level living and live out of our spirits. Our spirits are our vital union with God.

Confused means "being perplexed or disconcerted; disoriented with regard to a sense of one's time, place or identity; being disordered or mixed up." When you are perplexed you are "filled with uncertainty." Spiritually speaking, it feels like something is just not right. Some might call it a "check in your spirit." You just don't have a green light. You just don't have peace. You may not be able to put a finger on it. You just aren't settled in your spirit.

So what is peace? Merriam-Webster defines peace as "a state of tranquility or quiet; freedom from disquieting or oppressive thoughts or emotions." Oftentimes, a misgiven prophecy will not only give us a check in our spirit, it will open the door to disquieting or oppressive thoughts or emotions—especially if we accept it as true.

What Are You Meditating On?

Just like there is power in meditating on God's Word, there is power in meditating on other words. If we are meditating on false prophetic utterances, we are sowing those seeds in our hearts. We are renewing our mind to a false reality. Again, if the prophecy spoke to the idolatry in your heart, your soul might rejoice in it. But if you begin to feel a sense of confusion, uncertainty and the absence of peace, that's a good reason to question the source of the prophecy. When in doubt, always look to the written Word of God and submit it to others to judge.

Here's another important point: Ultimately, you need to be the one to bear witness with the word. Never, I repeat never, let someone force a prophetic word on you in the name of submitting to leadership. Jake was on staff at a church and felt the Lord leading

Him in a new direction. When he submitted what the Spirit of God was saying to him, the leadership of the church turned on him, one by one.

One prophesied that he had a 'python spirit' trying to take him out of his destiny. Another prophesied that he would be out of God's will if he left the church because there's only one church for every believer and he was already in his place. Another prophesied that he had a Jezebel spirit superimposed over his body. Others suggested he had a root of rebellion and pride. It seemed every staff member at the church had a different malady to prophesy or discern. If they were all right, this guy was a basket case who should never have been allowed in the pulpit. Of course, he also happened to be one of the biggest givers in the church, both financially and in terms of gifts and talents. Finally, the pastor told him he would lose his anointing if he left the ministry.

Did the Spirit of God say all that? Could this person who was preaching from the pulpit one day suddenly be found to have a python spirit and a Jezebel spirit attacking him, full of rebellion and pride? Is it possible that nobody saw it until he tried to move on? It's possible, but it's not likely, especially considering that it was his decision to leave that brought all the church prophets out of the woodwork with harsh words. The onslaught of prophetic words left Jake confused. He submitted those words to other pastors who debunked them using Scripture and some simple wisdom. Finally, the Lord told Him to move on and don't look back. When Jake obeyed, warfare broke out against him but he had the peace of God. God was trying to deliver him from a den of wolves.

Remember, there is a peace that comes from the world. Jesus said, "Peace I leave with you; My [own] peace I now give and bequeath to you. Not as the world gives do I give to you" (John 14:27 AMP). Don't be fooled by the peace that comes from the world. It comes with compromise. You are looking for peace in your spirit. Jesus can tell you what sounds like the most horrible news in the world to your soul, but you can still have peace in your spirit. Near the end of His journey on earth, Jesus spoke prophetically to His disciples. He told them that in a little while they would no longer see Him, and again after a short while they would see Him again (John 16:16). He told them that they would weep and grieve, but the world would rejoice; that they would be sorrowful, but their sorrow would be turned into joy (John 16:20). He compared the anguish they would feel to childbirth (John 16:21). That doesn't sound like good news, does it? But ultimately Jesus told them all these things so that they could maintain peace through the storm. The prophetic word sought to bring them peace.

> I have told you these things, so that in Me you may have [perfect] peace and confidence. In the world you have tribulation and trials and distress and frustration; but be of good cheer [take courage; be confident, certain, undaunted]! For I have overcome the world. [I have deprived it of power to harm you and have conquered it for you.]

> —John 16:33 (AMP)

Jesus' motive with this prophecy was so the disciples He loved so dearly would have not only peace, but the Amplified Bible says "perfect peace." And not only perfect peace, but also confidence. Also notice that Jesus prophesied the whole story. What if Jesus had merely said, "In a little while you will no longer see Me. You will weep and grieve. You will be sorrowful and feel the anguish of childbirth, and you won't be asking me for Me for anything anymore." Can you imagine? That would not have given the disciples much peace. It would have bred fear and confusion.

Prophetic ministers need to be careful to make sure they are telling the truth, the WHOLE truth, and nothing but the truth. I emphasize the whole truth here because my paraphrase above has truth in it—but it's not the whole truth. Jesus gave His disciples the whole truth, the bad, the ugly—and the good.

After Jesus was resurrected, He met with the disciples several times. A common greeting He used was, "Peace to you!" (John 20:19; John 20:21; John 20:26). At the beginning of many of Paul's epistles, he writes things like "Grace and spiritual blessing and peace be yours from God our Father and from the Lord Jesus Christ" (Romans 1:7 AMP). The Bible says the mind of the Holy Spirit is life and soul peace now and forever (Romans 8:6 AMP). One of the fruits of the Spirit is peace (Galatians 5:22).

Also consider that wisdom from God is first of all pure (undefiled); then it is peace-loving, courteous (considerate, gentile) (James 3:17 AMP). Peter said, "May grace (spiritual blessing) and peace be given you in increasing abundance [that spiritual peace to be realized in and through Christ, freedom from fears, agitating passions, and moral conflicts]"(1 Peter 1:2 AMP). Can you see God's peace agenda here?

If a prophecy causes confusion in your soul, and leaves you without peace, I'm not saying to throw it out completely. I'm just saying that the presence of confusion and the absence of peace should be red flag for you. You need to press into God and ask Him for the whole truth. But ultimately, if you remain confused and have no peace, stop meditating on the prophecy. If it's true, God will bring it back around with more clarity. If it's not, you don't need to spend your time meditating on it. Meditate on the written Word of God. If He wants to tell you something, He'll get through to you.

Pregnancy Confusion

A woman named Laura told me about a prophecy she received that caused her to run home in a hurry. Let's listen in:

> "My husband and I aren't planning on having kids, but a man I met told me, 'You will have a son, sooner than you think.' And he nodded at my stomach and indicated I was pregnant.

> "It ruined the party I was at because I was worrying about how my husband would react. So I ran home and did a pregnancy test straight away. Well … that was a couple of years ago."

Although Laura has received many prophetic words that did indeed come to pass, she was not pregnant and she has not had a baby to this day.

Why So Much Confusion?

There has been plenty of confusion in the Body of Christ over prophecy. Why? I think many times, especially in the realm of dreams and visions, the prophet just doesn't interpret what he's seeing correctly. Or, he may describe what he is seeing and you may interpret it wrong, which confuses you. So the dream or vision could be directly from the Lord, but we miss it in the interpretation. But don't worry. God is able to make Himself clear. I maintain that He's not trying to hide the truth from you. Seek the truth and you'll find the truth.

Sometimes the prophet doesn't remember all the details of a dream or vision. In this case, key parts may be left out that lead to confusion. This is why it's so important to write down the contents of dreams and visions right away. The same holds true when the "word of the Lord comes unto you saying." If you don't write it down, you could lose part of the essence of it and accidentally breed confusion.

So as we close this chapter, remember that the confusion test is designed to work in conjunction with judging the prophetic word against the written Word. It is possible that true words from the Lord could bring confusion, but I don't believe He intends them to. God is not the author of confusion, but of peace.

A Bona Fide Baby Prophecy

Not all prophecies about babies are goofy, erroneous, ambiguous or false. Many prophecies concerning marriage, babies and like topics are indeed of the Lord. Sara and Jimmy share the story of how they were praying for a child and a visiting pastor called them out to tell them they were going to have a child with a Joseph anointing.

"The pastor said God was going to give us a double blessing and that He would provide for all our needs. He said there is a strong anointing on one for song and on the other for the Word. Two years later I had twins and did not have to buy diapers for the first 18 months of their life!

Now, at two years old I already see that my son loves music and my daughter likes to talk and I know they are called and anointed. A few months ago a lady came to our church and came up to me and said, 'I don't know if you know it or not but your babies already have a very strong anointing on them.' Oh yes I know! Satan has tried two times to take out my little girl. I had to give her CPR at six weeks old. But she is going to fulfill the call. They both will, in Jesus name!"

CHAPTER 15

DOES THE PROPHECY BRING CONFIRMATION?

In the mouth of two or three witnesses shall

every word be established.

—2 Corinthians 13:1

Does the prophetic word compliment other prophetic words, counsel or spiritual insight from the Lord that you've received? Or does it take you off in another direction that seems contrary to everything you've known?

Yes, God could be shaking your world. But if God has consistently told you one thing and then another prophet comes up with something completely different for the same timeline, it's not likely both are accurate. Let me give you an example. Let's say God told you (and many prophetic people confirmed) that you are going to live in Miami and travel around the world preaching the Gospel for the next five years. Doors are starting to open. Suddenly, another prophet comes to town and says God has called you to move to New York and start a Bible college this year.

Given the timing, you need to question the source of that prophecy. It's possible (but unlikely) that both prophetic words are from God. With God, timing is everything. And sometimes prophets miss it when they put timelines on things. The word is generally true, but the timing element was inaccurate. It could be that God is both calling you to travel the world and start a Bible School. But perhaps not at the same time. Again, God's timing is vital.

When you are making major decisions about your life and ministry and you get conflicting words, you need to take the time to be certain what the Spirit if God is really saying. If something contradicts what you know that you know that you know in your spirit is true, then stick with your gut. God can correct you if you are wrong. Always remember, the Holy Ghost doesn't speak with a forked tongue. The Spirit of God doesn't speak out of both sides of His mouth. Jesus doesn't contradict Himself.

What is Confirmation?

Let's take a step back for a moment and be really clear about what we mean when we're talking about confirmation. A confirmation is a confirming proof. Merriam-Webster defines it as "the process of supporting a statement by evidence." Merriam-Webster defines evidence as, "one who bears witness."

Can you see it? Confirmation is evidence. And evidence is one who bears witness. Who bears witness? The Holy Spirit bears witness with our spirit that the prophetic word is true. Our proof comes not by what we see—your natural mind might not be able to comprehend how God could do this thing for, to or through you—but your proof comes from the Spirit of God who gives you peace in your spirit. You just know that you know that you know it is true.

Jesus confirmed He was the Christ over and over again by miracles, signs and wonders—and the religious leaders of the day still didn't believe He was who He said He was. We need to take caution in the prophetic. If God is trying to get the truth over to us and we keep denying the truth, how can we reach our destinies in Christ? Selah. When you hear the same prophetic word repeatedly, take heed. Be careful to judge it. If it confirms the truth that's already in your spirit, go for it. If you don't have any evidence, put it on the shelf or throw it in the trash.

Prophetic Announcements

There is such a thing as a prophetic announcement—something that you had no idea was coming. The Angel of the Lord made a prophetic announcement to Mary about Jesus (Luke 1:28-33). John the Baptist made a prophetic announcement about the coming of Christ (John 1:29). Samuel made a prophetic announcement over David's life (1 Samuel 16). An angel made a prophetic announcement to Gideon (Judges 6:12).

Prophetic announcements are a key part of prophetic ministry. God is able to do exceeding abundantly above all that we ask or think, according to the power that worketh in us (Ephesians 3:20). Since this is true, it follows that there are things God has planned for us that haven't even crossed our minds—and may even cause our minds to go tilt, tilt. That's why we don't ultimately judge prophecy with our soul (our mind, will and emotions). We discern true prophetic words spiritually. Our emotions can't be trusted in this realm, and our mind can reason things out too much, and our will can get in the way of what God wants to do sometimes. We discern prophetic words spiritually. The spiritual man makes judgments about all things (1 Corinthians 2:15).

So there are prophetic announcements. But more often prophetic words tend to confirm what we already know in our spirits, whether or not we've ever voiced it to anyone or even considered the reality of it. The prophecy may be a "now" word or speak of a time in the future, but it can still confirm what's already in your heart.

When you keep getting the same prophetic word from different people over and over, that often signals confirmation. But you should still judge it. The devil is more than capable of sending several people along your path to prophesy the idolatry in your heart or to deceive you into walking in a direction God has not planned. That's why I offer 27 ways to judge prophecy. If you judge a thing from multiple angles, you are more likely to see it for what it is. Ultimately, you need to be led by the Word and by the witness of the Spirit, but these other means of judging prophecy are good ways to flag a word when you can't find it in Scripture and you aren't discerning anything in your spirit.

Move in Faith

At the end of the day, you need to move in faith. Anything that is not of faith is sin (Romans 14:23). So if you make a move because a prophet confirmed something you thought was God—but you nevertheless still questioned it in your spirit—then how can you move in confidence? That's not pure faith. There's doubt mixed in there. Even if you did hear from God, with doubt in the mix you may not get the results you expected. Remember this: Faith is your confirmation.

> Now faith is the assurance (the confirmation, the title deed) of the things [we] hope for, being the proof of things [we] do not see and the conviction of their reality [faith perceiving as real fact what is not revealed to the senses].
>
> —Hebrews 11:1 (AMP)

I like to think of it this way: If your gift is prophecy, you are supposed to use your gift in proportion to your faith (Romans 12:6). We should receive prophecy the same way—according to the proportion of our faith. The Bible says faith comes by hearing the Word of God. So it reasons that if the prophetic word brings confirmation of the Word of God at work in your life, it will also stir faith.

PART 4

THE SPIRIT-BASED TESTS

The fruit of the Spirit is love, joy, peace, forbearance, kindness, goodness, faithfulness, gentleness and self-control. Against such things there is no law.

—Galatians 5:22-23 (NIV)

I've said it before and I'll say it again, and again, and again, and again. The Spirit and the Word agree. Say that out loud: The Spirit and the Word agree. The Word of God is Spirit-breathed. In other words, the Holy Spirit inspired the words on the pages of the Bible. So I refuse to believe that the Spirit of God will contract the Word of God. Father, Son and Holy Ghost are in perfect unity.

Being a student of the Word helps in the quest to accurately judge prophecy. We don't want to throw away a good word and we don't want to act on a bad word. But, again, everything we deal with in our lives isn't written on the pages of Scripture. Although there are principles we can apply to live victoriously, we do need guidance from the Holy Spirit—and the Bible promises that He will lead and guide us into all truth. One way He does that is through prophecy.

In Part 4 of our study, we're going to look at what I call the Spirit-Based Tests. Does your spirit bear witness to the prophetic word? Do other mature Christians bear witness to the utterance? Does the prophecy stir your spirit to pray and seek the Lord? Does it edify, comfort and exhort? Does the prophecy carry the fruit of the Spirit: love, joy, peace, forbearance, kindness, goodness, faithfulness, gentleness, and self-control?

These are all signposts that can alert you to true, erroneous or even false prophecies. Again, look at the prophecy through the lens of Scripture. You may not think the prophecy is loving, for example, but it may very well be. God corrects those whom He loves. The prophetic word may not necessarily put a burning desire in your heart to seek the Lord. That doesn't mean it's not true. I'm pointing out suggested ways to judge a word; to find another level of assurance of where the prophetic word originated. Think of it as looking at an diamond from all angles to make sure it's not a cubic zirconia. The Spirit-Based Tests offer some additional angles to help you be more confident of the prophecy's source.

CHAPTER 16

DOES YOUR SPIRIT BEAR WITNESS TO THE PROPHECY?

Ye have an unction from the Holy One, and ye know all things.
I have not written unto you because ye know not the truth, but
because ye know it, and that no lie is of the truth.

—1 John 2:20-21

Of all the signposts I've offered, this question is at the core of judging prophecy: Does your spirit bear witness to the prophetic word? Jesus promised that the Holy Spirit would lead and guide us into all truth (John 16:13). The Message translates that verse like this:

> But when the Friend comes, the Spirit of the Truth, he will take you by the hand and guide you into all the truth there is. He won't draw attention to himself, but will make sense out of what is about to happen and, indeed, out of all that I have

done and said. He will honor me; he will take from me and deliver it to you.

The Holy Spirit is the Spirit of Truth. One of His assignments is to lead and guide you into all truth. He'll take you by the hand and walk you toward the truth if the truth is what you want. He is the Truth-giving Spirit—and He dwells in your spirit.

> But you have been anointed by [you hold a sacred appointment from, you have been given an unction from] the Holy One, and you all know [the Truth] or you know all things. I write to you not because you are ignorant and do not perceive and know the Truth, but because you do perceive and know it, and [know positively] that nothing false (no deception, no lie) is of the Truth.
>
> —1 John 2:20-21 (AMP)

The truth doesn't breed lies. When you hear something that's "off" it should hit your spirit sideways. When you hear something that's true, it should settle in your heart with peace.

I always know when someone is lying to me. It just hits my spirit wrong. Why? Because the Spirit of God in me is omniscient. He knows everything. Since the Holy Spirit is dwelling in my spirit, if I remain sensitive to Him I will discern what pleases Him and what doesn't please Him. Lies don't please Him. So when someone is lying to me, I get a certain feeling in my spirit. I just know they aren't telling the truth. It's the same with prophecy. I just know when it's not true.

Paul put it this way, "I am speaking the truth in Christ. I am not lying; my conscience [enlightened and prompted] by the Holy Spirit bearing witness with me" (Romans 9:1 AMP). Your conscience is enlightened and prompted by the Holy Spirit. If you aren't picking up the inner witness of the Holy Spirit, then you may need to train your spirit to be more sensitive to His promptings.

CHAPTER 17

DO MATURE
CHRISTIANS BEAR WITNESS?

Two or three prophets should speak, and the others should weigh carefully what is said.

—1 Corinthians 14:29 (NIV)

When you are first learning to judge prophecy—or when the prophecy is directional—it's an especially good idea to let other mature Christians judge the prophetic word. Ultimately, you have to decide for yourself if it is true. There is safety in the counsel of many (Proverbs 11:14).

Maybe you are a baby Christian who doesn't have much experience being led by the Spirit. Or maybe you are a mature Christian who has never been exposed to the gifts of the Spirit in your denomination. Maybe you are seasoned in the prophetic but you are too close to a situation and your soul is running all over the place in reasonings, imaginations and emotions. It's usually a good idea to get other mature Christians to weigh carefully what is said.

Again, you need to be the one to decide whether or not you will accept or reject the prophetic word. If you feel pressured by other Christians to receive a word to which you don't bear witness, or if you feel pressure to submit every word about any aspect of your life for a leader's approval before you can accept it, you are out of balance and in danger of being deceived. You need to hear from the Lord for yourself, accepting the wise counsel of elders, but being careful not to be manipulated to do their bidding over God's.

My brothers and sisters, it's one thing to bring in your sweetheart to meet your pastor and ask him for his blessing before you get married. It's another thing altogether when you feel like you have to get permission from your pastor to get married to anyone; and that if your pastor says no you'll just crucify your flesh and move on even though you are certain God has brought you your mate. I'm not saying that we shouldn't take seriously the warnings of those who love us and may see things we don't. I'm just warning you against abuse of authority and prophetic manipulation.

Cindy's Sticky Situation

One young woman—we'll call her Cindy— wasn't sure if she could go on a missions trip with her local church. Cindy had gone every year for many years and really enjoyed going, but she had lost her job a year earlier and was still out of work. Even though she was living with her mother, her savings account was dwindling. Spending a couple of thousand dollars to travel to India for a week wasn't really in the budget. But she felt stuck between a rock and a hard place because she had some administrative skills the team always depended on during the missions. Cindy felt obligated, but the reality was she couldn't afford it and God was not providing the additional funds she needed. What's more, Cindy had just applied for a fantastic job where she had an inside connection. Being gone for a week could cause her to lose the opportunity to interview for the position that would turn her financial situation around and also give her an opportunity to continue her college education.

This is the kind of situation where you need the peace of God. You need to move in faith. You need to be certain of what God wants you to do. It could be that He wants you to trust Him and go on the mission, even though you would come home penniless. Or it could be that He wants you to put your house in order first, secure the job, and return to the mission field next year. There are always needs. There are always opportunities to serve on the mission fields. The question is this: Was God leading Cindy to go to the mission field or the job interview?

Cindy just didn't know what to do. She went back and forth on her decision and time was running out. So she went to one of the prophets in the local church who worked alongside the apostle on these annual events. She asked the prophet what he should do under the auspices of seeking confirmation. I believe that was a mistake and an open door for prophetic manipulation. God doesn't want us to be dependent on prophets for direction. He wants us to be dependent on Him.

Again, there's nothing wrong with getting counsel and submitting what you believe the Lord is saying to you. But there is a balance in this. When it gets out of balance one way or another, you either fall into the ditch of independence or the ditch of control. In other words, if you aren't willing to listen to and pray about the counsel you are given, you are in danger of getting stiff-necked and prideful. Pride comes before a fall. But if you allow other people to take the role of the Holy Ghost in your life, you are in danger of being manipulated and controlled by those who have an agenda that may or may not line up with God's will for you.

The Prophet's Motive

Back to Cindy's story…Cindy explained the situation to the prophet about the finances, about the job opportunity, and about her indecision. The prophet responded, "I just hear 'We need Cindy.'" Cindy decided to go on the mission trip based on that word because she respected the prophet. But she remained unsure about it every step of the way. She didn't have peace.

When Cindy told me about this, it really bothered me for a couple of reasons. First, Cindy needed to hear from God for herself. Second, I questioned whether this prophet was hearing the voice of God saying "We need Cindy" or whether that was part of the discussion in the staff meeting among the elder team: "We need Cindy!"

Something was out of line somewhere. Just weeks earlier, the apostle sat Cindy down from her administrative duties because she hadn't been faithful in attending the services. It was then discovered that had fallen into substance abuse, which is probably why she lost her last job. Cindy's responsibilities in the church were turned over to someone else. But when they needed someone who would pay to travel to a far away country and administrate the trip, suddenly Cindy was fit for service and "We need Cindy." It just didn't line up.

Perhaps what bothered me the most was that Cindy still didn't seem to have peace about going. She still seemed unsure when she told me, "I guess I am going to India after all." It's hard to have faith for the blessings of God if you aren't sure you are in His will. Cindy tried her best to believe for a breakthrough in India. But her faith was laced with doubt and tremendous financial stress. Cindy came back from the trip broke and did not get the job. In fact, the last time I spoke with Cindy she was still unemployed and living with her mother. The spiritual and natural fruit of following the prophet against her own peace was rotten.

CHAPTER 18

DOES THE PROHECY STIR YOURSPIRIT TO SEEK GOD?

The voice of the Lord echoes above the sea. The voice of the Lord is powerful. The voice of the Lord is majestic.

—Psalm 29

There's something about hearing the voice of God that stirs a hunger in you to draw nigh to Him. Perhaps it's the idea of the Creator of the Universe caring so much about us that He made His thoughts known to us. Or maybe it's a thankful heart to the kindness of God revealed that makes us hungry to be closer to Him. Maybe it's because we prophesy in part, and once we get one part we want to know the next part—so we seek Him.

Whatever the reason, many times a true prophetic word will leave us hungry for more parts! Prophecy should stir in us a hunger to pursue God's revealed will. Prophecy should cause us to pray and seek His timing, along with additional direction when necessary. Prophecy should stir us to study the Scriptures for additional insight. Prophecy should light a fire under us to take action. After all, faith without works is dead (James 2:20).

The Awesome Thoughts of the Lord

Consider the vivid language David used to describe the voice of the Lord in Psalm 29: "The voice of the Lord echoes above the sea. The voice of the Lord is powerful. The voice of the Lord is majestic. The voice of the Lord splits the mighty cedars. The voice of the Lord makes the barren wilderness quake. The voice of the Lord twists mighty oaks."

Although prophets aren't speaking with the voice of the Lord, they are uttering the thoughts of the Lord— and the thoughts of the Lord are powerful. When the thoughts of the Lord are spoken out through an anointed prophetic word, it should echo in your spirit, it should shake any wrong mindsets, it should stir in you a hunger to pursue Him.

The Bible says the counsel of the Lord stands forever, the thoughts of His heart to all generations (Psalm 33:11). The Bible also says, "Many, O Lord my God, are the wonderful works which You have done, and Your thoughts toward us; no one can compare with You! If I should declare and speak of them, they are too many to be numbered" (Psalm 40:5 AMP).

God's thoughts are profound (Psalm 92:5). His thoughts towards us are precious and great is the sum of them (Psalm 139:17). The Lord said, "For I know the thoughts that I think toward you, saith the Lord, thoughts of peace, and not of evil, to give you an expected end" (Jeremiah 29:11).

For my thoughts are not your thoughts, neither are your ways my ways. For as the heavens are higher than the earth, so are my ways higher than your ways, and my thoughts than your thoughts.

For as the rain cometh down, and the snow from heaven, and returneth not thither, but watereth the earth, and maketh it bring forth and bud, that it may give seed to the sower, and bread to the eater:

So shall my word be that goeth forth out of my mouth: it shall not return unto me void, but it shall accomplish that which I please and it shall prosper in the thing whereto I sent it.

—Isaiah 55:8-11

Considering all these Scriptures, I personally can't understand how a true prophetic word from the throne of heaven would not make somebody hungry for God—unless you just don't hold God's word in high esteem or unless you don't believe it came from the Lord. If the prophetic word carries truth, that truth should stir your spirit.

CHAPTER 19

DOES THE PROPHECY EDIFY, COMFORT OR EXHORT?

But he that prophesieth speaketh unto men to edification, and exhortation, and comfort.

—1 Corinthians 14:3

When you receive a prophetic word, it should primary edify, comfort or exhort you. If it doesn't do one or more of those three things, I would question the source of the prophecy. Since we have Scripture that tells us the purpose of the gift of prophecy (1 Corinthians 14:3), it makes it much easier to draw a discerning line in the sand. In fact, it doesn't even take someone with the gift of discernment to judge if a prophecy edifies, exhorts or comforts.

When I studied this out in Scripture, I was amazed at how much evidence there actually is for the case that prophecy should edify, comfort and exhort. Over and again there are examples in the Bible of prophecy and prophetic preaching and even Holy Ghost-inspired instruction to the Church that contains these elements. Over and again we are commended to edify, comfort and exhort one another. It's purely Scriptural.

Edification: To Build Up

Edification is a theme that runs across the New Testament. The word "edification" comes from the Greek word *oikodome*, meaning "to build up, establish, strengthen, to make effective."

Prophecy should edify the church. Paul put it this way: "I would that ye all spake with tongues but rather that ye prophesied: for greater is he that prophesieth than he that speaketh with tongues, except he interpret, that the church may receive edifying" (1 Corinthians 14:5). Paul also said, "Even so ye, forasmuch as ye are zealous of spiritual gifts, seek that ye may excel to the edifying of the church" (1 Corinthians 14:12). And again, "How is it then, brethren? when ye come together, every one of you hath a psalm, hath a doctrine, hath a tongue, hath a revelation, hath an interpretation. Let all things be done unto edifying" (1 Corinthians 14:26).

An intercessor named Linda tells me of a prophecy she received back in 1994. It's a good example of edification. As Linda describes it, the prophecy "gave her a boost."

"I was going through a time when I wondered if my prayers were really making a difference. I visited a little church in 1994, and the evangelist gave a word over me. The part that pierced deeply at the time was, 'Quietly and behind the scenes, shaping and forming in the Spirit, causing warriors to stand strong, and calling angels down to stand with.' The rest of the prophecy came to pass too, but over a period of years. That portion gave me a boost and I treasure it to this day."

Apostolic & Prophetic Authority

I want to take a moment to address the realm of apostolic and prophetic authority. Some camps within the Body of Christ have carried apostolic authority to the extreme while others refuse to accept it. The safest approach is to see how the New Testament apostles used their authority. The common denominator is edification. Consider the words of Paul the Apostle:

> I may seem to be boasting too much about the authority given to us by the Lord. But our authority builds you up; it doesn't tear you down. So I will not be ashamed of using my authority. I'm not trying to frighten you by my letters.
>
> —2 Corinthians 10:8-9 (NLT)

When Paul brought correction to the Corinthians, he wasn't trying to tear them apart. He was speaking the truth in love. He was trying to build them up in the faith of Christ. He wasn't trying to frighten them with his strong language. He was trying to stir them to repentance and a reverential fear of the Lord. That's true apostolic authority.

A True Spiritual Father

A young man named Bill once told me the story of how his apostle put such a demand on him to perform in service of the ministry that it caused him problems on the home front. His kids were unruly and resentful. His taxes were overdue. He never had time to visit his parents. The pressure to perform became so great that eventually, despite his best fleshly efforts, he couldn't keep up and he fell down on his volunteer ministry duties (which exceeded 30 hours a week).

The apostle put him on notice that he would be "sat down" if he didn't straighten up, so Bill worked harder. The apostle told him he'd be keeping a close eye on him. Well, Bill rose the occasion and performed at a high level in the ministry, though his family life and work continued to suffer. The apostle's response? "Congratulations. I didn't think you could do it. But you proved me wrong."

That's not the heart of a true apostle. Even with all the problems in the Corinthian church—and there were many, including divisions, carnality, immorality, fornication, abusing the Lord's supper, a lack of love, disorder, and wrong teachings about the resurrection of the dead—the Apostle Paul said this: "I have the highest confidence in you, and I take great pride in you. You have greatly encouraged me and made me happy despite all our troubles" (2 Corinthians 7:4). That's the heart of a true spiritual father.

Again, the purpose of Paul's bold words to the Corinthians is repeated here: "Therefore I write these things being absent, lest being present I should use sharpness, according to the power which the Lord hath given me to edification, and not to destruction" (2 Corinthians 13:10).

Do All Things Unto Edifying

Paul said we need to follow after the things which make for peace, and things wherewith one may edify another (Romans 14:19). How much more should the very word of the Lord edify us?

Paul said, "Let no corrupt communication proceed out of your mouth, but that which is good to the use of edifying, that it may minister grace unto the hearers" (Ephesians 4:29). How much more should the very word of the Lord edify us?

Paul said, "Neither give heed to fables and endless genealogies, which minister questions, rather than godly edifying which is in faith: so do" (1 Timothy 1:4). How much more should the very word of the Lord edify us?

Can you see it? Time and time again the Word leads us to edify one another. It's Satan who comes to tear us down. Yes, a prophetic word may work to root out, tear down and destroy certain wrong mindsets in a person's soul, but the prophetic word should not root out, tear down and destroy a person. That's not God.

Explaining Exhortation

The next element associated with the gift of prophecy is exhortation. The word "exhortation" comes from the Greek word *paraklesis*, meaning "a comforting encouragement provided in times of disappointment and affliction resulting in strengthening the resolve of the believer."

Pick up on those key words: comforting; encouragement; strengthening. Prophetic utterances should offer this flow. Oftentimes people ask me where warnings fall into the prophetic. I believe they are part and parcel of exhortation. When God wants to warn us of an enemy attack, He doesn't typically sound the alarm without offering some words of comforting encouragement to strengthen the resolve of the believer. When leading people into battle, God's M.O. is to assure them that He is with them. He exhorts them not to be afraid. Sometimes He'll give us a hint at the spoils of war. At the heart of exhortation is strengthening the believer to do God's will.

We can see exhortation in action across the New Testament. The church in Jerusalem sent forth Barnabus to exhort the believers in Antioch. Acts 11:23 says when he arrived and saw the evidence of the grace of God, he was glad and exhorted them all to remain true to the Lord with all their hearts. Judas and Silas, two prophets in the early church, exhorted the brethren with many words (Acts 15:32). These are examples of exhorting believers during a time when the church was facing persecution.

There are also New Testament examples of exhortation in the midst of affliction. When Paul, then a prisoner, was on his way to Rome in the midst of a storm, he exhorted the sailors to be of good cheer because there would be no loss of life, only the ship would be lost (Acts 27:22). Paul also exhorted believers to walk in a way that pleases God (1 Thessalonians 4:1) and to make supplications, prayers and intercessions for all men (1 Timothy 2:1). And Jude exhorted believers to contend for the faith (Jude 1:3).

Remember the definition of exhortation mentioned times of disappointment. When we are persecuted, afflicted, disappointed or otherwise struggling, one word of prophecy can exhort us to keep standing. One word from the Lord can change our entire perspective on the situation we are in. One prophetic utterance can shift our mindsets and cause us to hold on a little tighter. Prophetic exhortation is a godsend.

Calling for Comfort

Finally, prophecy should bring comfort. The word "comfort" comes from the Greek word *paramuthia*, meaning "to provide a freedom from worry during times of grief, affliction or distress and bringing assurance to the believer."

Jesus said, "Blessed are they that mourn: for they shall be comforted" (Matthew 5:4). Sometimes the Lord decides to comfort us through a prophetic word that assures us everything is going to be alright. Comfort is a key New Testament theme.

The Holy Spirit Himself is called the Comforter (John 14:16; John 14:26; John 15:26). And our Heavenly Father is the God of all comfort (2 Corinthians 1:3). So it makes sense that His words to us would bring comfort. It makes sense that He would comfort those that are cast down (2 Corinthians 7:6) with His words. It's only natural that He should comfort our hearts and establish us in every good word and work (2 Thessalonians 2:17).

The Apostle Paul said, "For ye may all prophesy one by one, that all may learn, and all may be comforted" (1 Corinthians 14:31). Prophecy often has an element of comfort in it. Comfort runs hand in hand with edification and exhortation. This Spirit-inspired trio undergirds true prophecy.

CHAPTER 20

IS THE PROPHECY LOVING?

And many false prophets shall rise, and shall deceive many. And because iniquity shall abound, the love of many shall wax cold. But he that shall endure unto the end, the same shall be saved.

—Matthew 24:11-13

Prophecy should find its source in love—because it comes from God who is love. I find it especially interesting that Jesus connected the ability of false prophets to deceive many with love growing cold. It's almost like people are numb to the truth because they are numb to Love, which is God, which is Truth.

God loved us so much that He gave His only begotten Son, that whosoever believeth in Him should not perish, but have everlasting life (John 3:16). God commendeth His love toward us, in that, while we were yet sinners, Christ died for us (Romans 5:8). Everything God gives us is motivated by and rooted in love. Therefore, so should prophetic words be.

What eye has not seen and ear has not heard and has not entered into the heart of man, [all that] God has prepared (made and keeps ready) for those who love Him [who hold Him in affectionate reverence, promptly obeying Him and gratefully recognizing the benefits He has bestowed].

Yet to us God has unveiled and revealed them by and through His Spirit, for the [Holy] Spirit searches diligently, exploring and examining everything, even sounding the profound and bottomless things of God [the divine counsels and things hidden and beyond man's scrutiny].

—1 Corinthians 2:9-10 (AMP)

God loves us so much that we can't even imagine what good things He has prepared for us. He reveals them by His Spirit—and many times through prophetic words. How can prophecy not find its origins in love? I submit to you that false prophecy is not rooted in love, but rather some other motive. The love of money is the root of all evil and is the root of some false prophecy that sets out to wring the cash from your pocketbook. Remember, the fruit of the Spirit is love…(Galatians 5:22). So if the prophecy is coming from the Holy Spirit, love will be among its fruit.

Control, Correction & Condemnation

Control is not one of the characteristics of love. The Holy Ghost doesn't control us. He is a gentleman. It grieves Him when misguided prophets use the influence afforded them as a mouthpiece of God to deliver adulterated prophetic words, curses, or other controlling or fearful utterances.

What about words of correction? Sometimes the Holy Spirit speaks to me and I say, "Ouch." Yes, the Holy Spirit convicts. "For whom the Lord loveth he chasteneth, and scourgeth every son whom he receiveth" (Hebrews 12:6). But false or erroneous prophecy goes beyond conviction to condemnation.

The Lord told me how to tell the difference between the His conviction and the devil's condemnation: by understanding His love. Even God's correction can bring peace to your spirit. Prophetic words laced in condemnation will only bring guilt and torment. Remember, "There is no fear in love; but perfect love casteth out fear: because fear hath torment. He that feareth is not made perfect in love" (1 John 4:18).

PART 5

THE CHARACTER TESTS

Therefore select out from among yourselves, brethren, seven men of good and attested character and repute, full of the [Holy] Spirit and wisdom, whom we may assign to look after this business and duty.

—Acts 6:3 (AMP)

Jesus said we would know people by their fruit. But looking at the fruit of a ministry is not enough. We must look at character, which should be ever-ripening without rotting.

Think about Jesus, the Prophet. He is our prototype Prophet and His testimony is the spirit of prophecy (Revelation 19:10). Jesus didn't seek His own will. He sought the will of the Father who sent Him (John 6:38). Doubtless, being committed to the will of the Father was much easier for Him when He was casting out devils and prophesying, but He stuck to His guns even to the point of blood. So must modern-day prophets.

I've heard some say that character issues don't matter in the prophetic. Such statements floor me. The

Lord doesn't expect prophets to be perfect, but He does expect prophets to be willing to look at themselves in the mirror of the Word and allow the Holy Spirit to convict them of sin so the blood of Jesus can cleanse them from all unrighteousness. That requires humility of heart and a willingness to lay aside childish things and walk worthy of the prophetic vocation.

In Part 5 of our study, we're going to examine with great caution the character of the prophetic vessel. This is done with a mind toward judging prophetic words, not judging the prophet. But if the vessel is full of darkness, we must take caution in receiving any utterances from that vessel just as we would take caution about eating out of a bowl with mold growing around the edges.

CHAPTER 21

DOES THE PROPHET
EXALT HIMSELF?

Now the man Moses was very meek (gentle, kind, and humble)
or above all the men on the face of the earth.

—Numbers 12:3 (AMP)

The only prophet that we should exalt is Jesus. Yet too often in the Body of Christ we exalt men to rock star prophetic status. When we do that, we are in danger of walking through the doorway of deception. Prophets should be exalting Jesus, not themselves. And not just in word. Don't be fooled. It's easy enough to lift up Jesus through one side of your mouth and lift yourself up through the other. It's an awesome responsibility to walk in the prophetic, but true prophets seek to walk in humility that glorifies the Lord.

Every prophet should be cooperating with the grace of God to walk in humility. Moses walked in humility. In fact, the Bible says he was the meekest man on earth—yet we know he wasn't perfect. The prophet doesn't need to have perfect humility; just a perfect heart toward God. We all have unperceived pockets of pride in our lives and we will until we shed these fleshly bodies. But there's a marked difference between one who is making an effort to walk in humility and one who follows his pride. We should look for the fruit of meekness in the prophet's life. It's a character issue that's vital to true prophetic ministry.

I might add that there's also a difference between arrogance and confidence. The arrogant prophet puts his trust in himself. The confident prophet puts his trust in Christ. The arrogant prophet carries insecurities about who he is in Christ. The confident prophet is secure in his identity. A confident prophet can admit when he misses it and seeks the Lord for clarification to avoid making the same mistake again. The arrogant prophet refuses to admit that he missed it and brags about his track record. Get the picture?

Casting Down Prophetic Exaltation

The Bible says we should cast down imaginations, and every high thing that exalts itself against the knowledge of God (2 Corinthians 10:5). In my opinion, we should cast down prophetic words that exalt the prophet who delivers them. But that doesn't always happen. Even Paul saw Spirit-filled Christians putting up with false ministers spewing false doctrine:

> For such are false apostles, deceitful workers, transforming themselves into the apostles of Christ. And no marvel; for Satan himself is transformed into an angel

of light. Therefore it is no great thing if his ministers also be transformed as the ministers of righteousness; whose end shall be according to their works.

I say again, let no man think me a fool; if otherwise, yet as a fool receive me, that I may boast myself a little. That which I speak, I speak it not after the Lord, but as it were foolishly, in this confidence of boasting. Seeing that many glory after the flesh, I will glory also.

For ye suffer fools gladly, seeing ye yourselves are wise. For ye suffer, if a man bring you into bondage, if a man devour you, if a man take of you, if a man exalt himself, if a man smite you on the face.

—2 Corinthians 11:13-20

Don't readily receive prophetic words from apostles and prophets—or any other ministry—who exalts himself or herself. It's one thing for God to exalt a prophet who has humbled himself. It's quite another for the prophet to exalt himself—and especially to speak forth words in the name of prophecy that exalt him or his ministry. Again, let's remember that Moses, a true prophet of God, was the meekest man on earth in his day (Numbers 12:3). Humility is the hallmark of a true prophet. Self-exaltation has its roots in self and is an earmark of self-deception.

CHAPTER 22

DOES THE PROPHECY
PRESSURE YOU TO GIVE?

*For the love of money is the root of all evil: which while some
coveted after, they have erred from the faith, and pierced
themselves through with many sorrows.*

—1 Timothy 6:10

You've probably been in a church service—or watched
one on TV—where the preacher has come up with
some sort of creative way to link an offbeat Bible story
to giving. I submit to you that there are plenty of
stories in the Bible about giving without having to twist
Scripture to make your point. These prophetic
preachers passionately and convincingly explain how
the Lord showed them a newfangled sowing strategy as
they labored in prayer unto your breakthrough.

Some of these money-hungry ministers take a
Scripture and connect it to a dollar amount the Lord
has commanded "all those within the sound of my

voice" to give in order to receive a supernatural harvest. One that I've often seen used "prophetically" is Luke 6:38. Luke 6:38 says, "Give, and it will be given to you. A good measure, pressed down, shaken together and running over, will be poured into your lap. For with the measure you use, it will be measured to you." So the prophetic preacher assures you that if you sow $638 dollars right away, you can see this promise come to pass in your life before the end of the month. Or you can opt for the payment plan and split that amount up over 12 months. There are variations on this false prophetic promise. Yes, the Scripture itself is true, but the application of the Scripture is often twisted in the name of prophecy and to the benefit of the preacher.

The root of these types of financial directives could be greed, but it could also be desperation to pay ministry bills. Greed is selfish and excessive desire for more of something—oftentimes money—than is needed. Yes, God is a God of more than enough and we should want more than enough so we can help others who don't have enough. We should want to be blessed in abundance so we can be an abundant blessing. That's not greed. Greed is when you want more than you need because you are just plain selfish. Greed may also be a manifestation of distrust in God as your Provider. In any case, the greedy prophet wants to horde cash to himself to supply all his needs according to his own deceitful riches in vain glory. And the desperate prophet simply isn't trusting God to sustain his ministry. But let's focus on greed for a moment.

Blind, Ignorant Watchmen

The Bible has plenty to say about the greedy man. Greedy prophets lay wait and lurk privily (Proverbs 1:18-20). The Message Bible translation says they are "racing to a very bad end, hurrying to ruin everything they lay hands on, and robbing a bank while everyone is watching." Greedy prophets trouble their own house (Proverbs 15:27). And Isaiah offers a horrifying look at the greedy watchman. As you read this Scripture, keep in mind that part of the prophetic post is to serve as a watchman.

> His watchmen are blind: they are all ignorant, they are all dumb dogs, they cannot bark; sleeping, lying down, loving to slumber. Yea, they are greedy dogs which can never have enough, and they are shepherds that cannot understand: they all look to their own way, every one for his gain, from his quarter.
>
> —Isaiah 56:10-11

What good is a blind, ignorant prophet who can't sound the alarm? I believe greed—the lust of the eyes—blinds us to what the Spirit of the Lord is really saying and doing because it's filtered through a desire for profit. Greedy prophets aren't seeing or saying right. Their utterances are muddied by their insatiable desire for their own way and their own gain. They misinterpret—or flat out fabricate—what the Lord is saying because their ears are full of cha-ching sounds that drown out all else.

Ezekiel hits the same greedy spirit, rebuking those who "hast greedily gained of thy neighbors by extortion" (Ezekiel 22:11). Extortion isn't only for gun-toting Mafiosos with pin-stripped suits and Italian accents like we see in gangster movies of old. Extortion means to obtain from a person by force, intimidation, or undue illegal power—or to gain especially by ingenuity or compelling argument. In other words, extortion can be charismatically subtle. Greedy prophets misuse their power—they use undue illegal power—to wring money from your wallet.

It seems some prophets and prophetic camps believe they have a monopoly on the word of the Lord. I've spoken to some so-called apostles and prophets one-to-one, ear-to-ear, who have boldly told me things like, "Prophet So-and-So proclaimed this and such and we are not to question it." Others seem to believe that if they pronounce it the rest of the Body of Christ should not only agree without judging the utterance, but should also support it financially—and liberally. Still other prophets expect exorbitant honorariums for their exhortations, tainted as they often are.

Don't get me wrong, I believe in offering honorariums to visiting ministers and supporting our men and women of God in the local church, but demanding exceedingly exorbitant honorariums, limousines and travel expenses for your whole company seems a bit much in exchange for bringing forth the Word of the Lord. Jesus said we have received freely and we should give freely (Matthew 10:8). Honorariums are often appropriate, but greedy demands are not. Jesus warned against greed:

Guard yourselves and keep free from all covetousness (the immoderate desire for wealth, the greedy longing to have more); for a man's life does not consist in and is not derived from possessing overflowing abundance or that which is over and above his needs.

—Isaiah 56:10-11 AMP

One Root of False Prophecy

When the Apostle Paul outlined the qualifications of a minister of the Gospel to his spiritual son Timothy, he twice mentioned the need to be greed-free. Specifically, he made it clear that a minister should not be "greedy of filthy lucre" (1 Timothy 3:3, 8). The Amplified Bible says a minister should not be a "lover of money [insatiable for wealth and ready to obtain it by questionable means]" and the Message Bible translation flat out says we shouldn't be "money-hungry."

You can't be money-hungry and Spirit-hungry at the same time. You can't serve both God and mammon (Matthew 6:24). I know this is Christianity 101, but if the lust of the eyes—greed—wasn't an effective strategy against prophets, then the Bible wouldn't repeatedly warn us about it. Greed is dangerous because it opens the door to other sins such as envy, covetousness and merchandising. Watch out for greedy prophets!

CHAPTER 23

WHAT IS THE CONSISTENT CHARACTER OF THE PROPHET?

For even the Son of man came not to be ministered unto, but to minister, and to give his life a ransom for many.

—Mark 10:45

Nobody is perfect. We're certainly not going on a prophetic witch hunt in this chapter that discusses the importance of the character of the vessel that delivers the thoughts of God. We're just looking for the consistent character of the prophet. Of course, that's a little more difficult to do when the prophet is a visiting minister from another church.

You can always check on the background of the prophet, but what you find could be incorrect. There are plenty of wonderful men and women of God, for example, who are smeared on the Internet by false accusations. And sometimes prophets with poor character seem to be glamorized by those with itching ears. So what is a believer to do?

Bill Hamon's Ten Ms

Bill Hamon, founder of Christian International, offers what he calls the "10 Ms" for maturing and maintaining prophetic ministry. These serve as a good basic outline for examining the character of the prophet. I would highly suggest picking up Dr. Hamon's books and CDs on this topic, but will offer a brief outline to give you a taste of his teaching. Some of these issues we've already touched on in other parts of this chapter.

1. Manhood: Is the prophet the man or woman that God intends for them to be in Christ?

2. Ministry: Does the prophet demonstrate love and grace?

3. Message: Does the prophet speak the truth in love, avoiding extremes and sticking close to Scripture?

4. Maturity: Does the prophet carry a godly attitude of worship in relationships?

5. Marriage: Is the prophet's house in order? Do they put God first, then family, then ministry?

6. Methods: Are the prophet's methods of ministry ethical and honest rather than manipulative and controlling?

7. Manners: Does the prophet have good manners? Are they self-less, preferring others?

8. Money: Does the prophet have a love for money or improper stewardship of finances?

9. Morality: Does the prophet live a pure lifestyle? Do they take the high road in all areas?

10. Motive: Is the prophet's motive to be seen of men or to serve men?

True prophets are servants of God and man, not servants of self or money. If the prophet's character is consistently and visibly lacking in several of Dr. Hamon's 10 Ms, I would proceed with great caution in receiving that ministry. Again, nobody is perfect. We're not talking about mistakes. We're talking about practicing a lifestyle that is not godly—and refusing to yield to the Spirit of God to change.

CHAPTER 24

DOES THE PROPHECY REBUKE OR CORRECT?

Preach the word! Be ready in season and out of season. Convince, rebuke, exhort, with all longsuffering and teaching.

—2 Timothy 4:2 (NJKV)

Should prophecy publicly rebuke, correct or reveal negative personal information? There are two camps in the Body of Christ. One will answer yes and the other will answer no.

The Bible indicates leaders in the Church should use Scripture to rebuke (2 Timothy 3:16-17; 2 Timothy 4:2). I also believe there are true rebukes of the Spirit. But I don't think it's commonplace, especially in a public setting. God is long-suffering and full of grace and mercy.

I've seen people living in sin and they just seem to get away with it. They continue to receive prophetic words of blessing, and yet they don't change their sinful habits. I don't condone practicing sin in any way shape or form—and neither does God. I believe there comes a time to address sin, but I believe God gives a person every opportunity to do so privately before taking it public. Even if the Spirit of God does take it public, His motive is love because He desperately wants to get through to the person.

We know that Paul rebuked Syntyche, Hymanaeus, Euodia, Alexander and Philetus. We know that John rebuked Diotrophes. We see other apostles rebuking people who were propagating false doctrines, but they are not mentioned specifically by name. (If they read the letter, though, they'd probably know it was about them.) What's different about those public rebukes is that they weren't delivered as a prophetic word. Yes, the Scripture is inspired by the Holy Spirit. But these people weren't standing in a prayer line, expecting to receive something that would help them fight the good fight of faith—only to get hit with a public rebuke preceded by "thus saith the Lord."

I've heard leaders who were insecure about their dwindling church attendance proclaim things from the pulpit like, "I'm tired of people dragging people out of this church. If this doesn't stop, I'm going to start naming names." That sort of fear-laced threat did not originate from the Spirit of God. God doesn't operate through fear. Perhaps people are leaving because the leadership is flowing in a wrong spirit.

I've also heard leaders say, "If you leave this ministry, you'll lose your anointing. For 25 years I've watched people try to leave here and start their own ministry. They always fail. You succeed here because of the anointing on the house. You won't succeed without me." This is another fear and control tactic with a predictive edge. It's not the Holy Spirit, and it's not delivered as prophecy, but it's a fearful prediction by the same man of God who stands before the congregation to preach, pray and prophesy. Essentially, it's a curse. This is a problem.

Keep it Private

I believe if any leader needs to correct any believer, he should first do it privately. In fact, Scripture confirms this approach: "If your brother sins against you, go and show him his fault, just between the two of you. If he listens to you, you have won your brother over" (Matthew 18:15 NIV). This is a principle. You could apply it to sin against you or sin against someone else. If you see the sin and the Holy Spirit inspires you to address it, the first line is to do it privately. I believe prophetic words that address sin should not be loosely delivered in a public setting.

We see that God is not hasty about exposing sin publicly by the next verse: "But if he will not listen, take one or two others along, so that 'every matter may be established by the testimony of two or three witnesses'" (Matthew 18:16 NIV). This approach still contains the knowledge of the sin to less than a handful of people. God's preferred method of correction is to get the believer to repent, not shame him publicly. Shame is the devil's domain.

There does come a time, though, when the matter escalates. "If he refuses to listen to them, tell it to the church; and if he refuses to listen even to the church, treat him as you would a pagan or a tax collector" (Matthew 18:17 NIV). If the entire church judges the matter the same way, it becomes a form of godly peer pressure that hopes to lead the person to repent. If that doesn't work, we stop fellowshipping with the one who is practicing sin, yet we don't curse or condemn him. We walk in love with him just as we do with lost souls, but we withdraw our fellowship.

With these instructions in mind, it reasons that prophetic words that publicly aim to call a person out without having first attempted to address the issue privately don't line up with Scripture.

Then there's 1 Timothy 5:20 that says, "Do not receive an accusation against an elder except on the basis of two or three witnesses. Those who continue in sin, rebuke in the presence of all, so that the rest also will be fearful of sinning" (I Timothy 5:20-21). Again, this is not speaking of prophecy, but does set the stage for the possibility of a true public rebuke of the Spirit.

My thoughts are this: A prophet should not take pleasure in exposing the sin of another publicly. If a prophet receives a word of rebuke, he or she should take that word to the person's leader, let the presbytery judge it, and then, if necessary, address it with the believer. The prophet could be completely, 100 percent wrong—but when the utterance is spoken in front of a congregation it maligns the character of the believer. That is completely out of line with God's will, it can bring great confusion and fear, and it can even turn some away from God.

The Heart's Motive

You always have to look at the motive behind the prophecy. False prophets are murderous, maligning the reputation of others to make themselves look good. It's one thing to call a sin a sin. It's another thing to assassinate someone's character for your own gain.

This can be a thin line indeed. The Spirit—not a spirit—but the Spirit of God must lead us.

Again, we know that the Apostle Paul warned Timothy of false teachers. He also let Timothy know that Demas deserted him because "he loved this present world" (2 Timothy 4:10). He also singled out Alexander the metalworker who did him harm and warned Timothy to "be on your guard against him because he strongly opposed our message" (2 Timothy 4:14-15). Even John, the Apostle of Love, warned of Diotrephes, who "loves to be first" and was gossiping maliciously about John and his company (3 John 1:9-10).

Prophets should warn the church of those who are hell bent on destroying God's work and perverting His voice. But it's the spirit behind the announcement that needs to be judged. I believe that most often we can call out the deceived among the Body of Christ without naming names. I believe it's enough to describe the actions and teach the truth—and then only as the Spirit of God leaves. No heresy hunting. Do you know how they teach bankers to discern a counterfeit $100 bill? It's not by having them study counterfeit bills, as you would think. Rather, it's by having them study authentic bills.

CHAPTER 25

IS THE PROPHET PART OF A LOCAL CHURCH?

And God has appointed these in the church: first apostles, second prophets, third teachers, after that miracles, then gifts of healings, helps, administrations, varieties of tongues.

—1 Corinthians 12:28 NKJV

In the Old Testament, we often see prophets going from assignment to assignment delivering prophetic words. This would be the modern-day equivalent to the itinerant minister. But in the New Testament, God expects prophets to be an active part of the local church, even if they do travel quite a bit. We see this repeatedly in Scripture.

> And God hath set some in the church, first apostles, secondarily prophets, thirdly teachers, after that miracles, then gifts of healings, helps, governments, diversities of tongues.
>
> —1 Corinthians 12:28

No matter what translation you read, you can't get away from the fact that God set prophets in the church. The NIV says, "And in the church God has appointed first of all apostles, secondarily prophets…" The New Living Translation confirms, "Here are some of the parts God has appointed for the church, first are apostles, second are prophets…" And The Message says, "You're familiar with some of the parts that God has formed in his church, which is his 'body'…"

A Call for Spiritual Accountability

There is no such thing as an independent prophet. The apostolic is about teams. Even the Lone Ranger worked with Tonto. Batman worked with Robin. You get the picture. Prophets are part of the foundation of the Church (Ephesians 2:20) that are set in the Church to perfect the saints for the work of the ministry, along with apostles, evangelists, pastors and teachers (Ephesians 4:11).

Yes, a prophet can be an itinerant minister. But the prophet should still have a home church where he or she has accountability to other spiritual leaders. If the prophet is not accountable to anyone, that should send up a red flag.

What's more, you can't rent a spiritual father. You can't buy into a network and receive a "covering." True spiritual accountability, which is vital in this hour, comes out of balanced, healthy relationships where the spiritual mentors have the best interests of their spiritual mentees at heart, and the prophet knows they will be held accountable for irresponsible behavior.

CHAPTER 26

DOES THE PROPHET
TRY TO GET YOU ALONE?

For neither at any time used we flattering words, as ye know, nor a cloke of covetousness; God is witness.

—1 Thessalonians 2:5

You've probably heard of the parking lot prophet. This is the guy who wants to prophesy to you privately. Sometimes he'll pull you into a quiet corner of the church to tell you "thus saith the Lord." Other times he'll follow you to your car—in the parking lot. Still other times he'll call you on the phone with his dark sayings.

Beware of prophets who want to deliver their prophetic utterances to you in private. Sure, it could be something of a sensitive nature. So this alone isn't an end all means of judging prophecy. We know Matthew 18 commands us to address a brother who has sinned against us privately. But when someone wants to deliver a prophetic word in private it should cause you to take caution—especially if you don't know the person. If you do have a strong relationship with the prophet, and the prophet has strong character, then there is no harm in receiving a prophetic word privately. But you should still write it down.

If a prophet you don't know tells you he has a word for you, ask him to write it down so you can read it at home later in a quiet place. If he isn't willing to write it down, then that should be a red flag to you. He may be concerned about being held accountable for what he has written in the name of the Lord. If the prophet insists on delivering the word to you, grab somebody—anybody—as a witness. That could cause the prophet to clam up quick if he has foul motives.

CHAPTER 27

ARE YOU DEALING
WITH A FALSE PROPHET?

For false Christs and false prophets shall rise, and shall shew signs and wonders, to seduce, if it were possible, even the elect.

—Matthew 7:13-14

I don't believe false prophets start off as false prophets. I believe they start off on the right track, with zeal and fervor for the Lord, with a hunger for His voice, and with a determination to build the Kingdom of God. Unfortunately, some genuine, God-called prophets end up on the road of deception.

The matter of recognizing false prophets is a subject for another book. In fact, I deal with this issue extensively in my book, "A Prophet's Heart." If you are in prophetic ministry, I would recommend that you read that book as well as my other work, "The Heart of the Prophetic."

Suffice it to say that a false prophet is not merely someone who delivers an inaccurate word. A false prophet is someone who sets out to deceive, and is himself deceived. False prophets are running rampant through the Body of Christ to steal, kill and destroy God's work. These people are deceived. Many of think they are following the Spirit of God, but they are following evil spirits.

Warnings About False Prophets

I believe we can discern the false even quicker by studying true prophets and their character, and I also believe we need to teach about what false prophets look like and call out their falsehoods.

So let's look at a few earmarks of a false prophet according to Scripture. Noteworthy is the fact that false apostles, prophets and teachers are mentioned repeatedly throughout the New Testament. Jesus addressed it. Paul addressed it. Peter addressed it. John addressed it. You can hardly read a book in the New Testament without a warning about false ministers or false doctrine. Here are a few references.

> For there shall arise false Christs, and false prophets, and shall show great signs and wonders; insomuch that, if it were possible, they shall deceive the very elect (Matthew 24:24).

Beware of false prophets, which come to you in sheep's clothing, but inwardly they are ravening wolves (Matthew 7:15).

And many false prophets shall rise, and shall deceive many (Matthew 24:11).

And when they had gone through the isle unto Paphos, they found a certain sorcerer, a false prophet, a Jew, whose name was Barjesus (Acts 3:19).

But there were false prophets also among the people, even as there shall be false teachers among you, who privily shall bring in damnable heresies, even denying the Lord that bought them, and bring upon themselves swift destruction (2 Peter 2:1).

Beloved, believe not every spirit, but try the spirits whether they are of God: because many false prophets are gone out into the world (1 John 4:1).

Signs of False Prophets

Let me leave you with a list of characteristics of false prophets found in Scripture, both the Old Testament and the New Testament.

- Merchandisers
- Dishonest
- Lack a fear of the Lord
- Smooth flattering prophecies
- Thieving
- Strife and division
- Questionable prophecies
- Adulterous
- Immoral
- Drunken
- Presumptuous
- Unaccountable
- Greedy
- Lying
- Slanderers
- Profane
- Con artists, tricksters and frauds
- Self-centered, autocratic, unethical
- Avoid confronting sin
- Love money and support lavish, extravagant lifestyles
- Celebrity, stardom and preeminence
- Unsociable, cold, aloof
- Malicious, slanderous, venomous, gossips

- Discontent and Dissatisfied
- Isolate and separate
- Seeking prestige
- Controlling manipulators, workers of witchcraft

When you see ministers practicing these things, run the other direction. Yes, everybody makes mistakes, but there's a difference between making a mistake and practicing sin. The Holy Ghost convicts us of sin, but if we ignore Him repeatedly our conscience becomes seared and we get dull of hearing.

CHAPTER 28

IS THE PROPHECY DELIVERED IN ANGER OR JUDGMENT?

Love suffers long and is kind; love does not envy; love does not parade itself, is not puffed up; does not behave rudely, does not seek its own, is not provoked, thinks no evil; does not rejoice in iniquity, but rejoices in the truth; bears all things, believes all things, hopes all things, endures all things.
Love never fails.

—1 Corinthians 13:4-8

God is a God of grace. He's not sitting on His throne, angry and looking for the first opportunity to use a prophet to heap judgment on you. He's really not. Knowing that God is patient and kind, that He does not envy and does not boast, that He is not proud, that He is not rude or self-seeking, not easily angered and keeps no record of wrongs—knowing this it is difficult to accept as true a prophecy delivered in a spirit of anger and judgment.

The spirit of prophecy is the testimony of Jesus (Revelation 19:10). What was Jesus' testimony while He walked the earth? Did he have angry judgment toward sinners? Or did He seek to save those who were lost? Did He condemn the world? Or did He die to save it?

Again, the majority of personal prophecy should edify, exhort or comfort. It's hard to imagine an angry, judgmental prophet edifying, exhorting or comforting anyone. God's spiritual gifts are born out of love. He gave His gifts to the church to express His love, not His anger and not His judgment.

Yes, there is righteous indignation. But that is different than soulish anger. Man's anger does not bring about the righteous life that God desires (James 1:20 NIV). True prophecy should lead you that righteous life.

AFTERWORD

In conclusion, I leave you with this Scripture: "Do not treat prophecies with contempt. Test everything. Hold on to the good. Avoid every kind of evil" (1 Thessalonians 5:20-22). Don't let some inaccurate or even false prophecies turn you away from prophetic ministry. Just learn to judge prophecy, hold fast to the good words and disregard the bad ones, praying for the prophet who delivered it.

What's more, "Judge not according to the appearance, but judge righteous judgment (John 7:24). I've said repeatedly through this work that prophecy needs to stay in line with the Spirit of the Word of God. You may not be able to find Chapter and Verse to line up with a prophecy you received, but you can discern if the prophetic word agrees with the ways of the Spirit of God. The better you know God and His ways—and are submitted to Him—the less chance you have to fall into deception.

When in doubt, pray it out. If God gave the prophet a word for you and you aren't sure, take it to God. He will confirm whether it was Him or not through the witness of the Holy Spirit in your spirit and with peace.

Let me put it another way. You can't judge prophecy based on experiences and manifestations, emotions, how large is the crowd that follows someone's ministry, the testimony of others who say the prophet is accurate, apparent financial prosperity, or charisma. You have to judge prophecy according to the Word, the witness of the Spirit, the fruit of the prophetic word, the clarity of the word and the character of the one delivering it. Always remember, the Word and the Spirit agree. Amen.

ABOUT THE AUTHOR

Jennifer LeClaire is a prophetic voice and teacher whose passion is to see the lost come to Christ and equip believers to understand the will and ways of God. She carries a reforming voice that seeks to turn hearts to the Lord and edify the Body of Christ.

Jennifer has a powerful testimony of God's power to set the captives free and claim beauty for ashes. She shares her story with women who need to understand the love and grace of God in a lost and dying world.

Jennifer is the news editor at *Charisma* magazine. She writes a weekly column called "The Plumb Line." Some of her work is archived in the Flower Pentecostal Heritage Museum.

Jennifer is a prolific author who has written several books, including "The Heart of the Prophetic," "A Prophet's Heart," "Doubtless: Faith that Overcomes the World," "Fervent Faith: Discover How a Fervent Spirit is a Defense Against the Devil" and "Breakthrough" Her materials have been translated into Spanish and Korean.

Other Books by Jennifer LeClaire

The Heart of the Prophetic: Keys to flowing in a more powerful prophetic anointing

A Prophet's Heart: Avoiding the Doorway to Deception

Doubtless: Faith that Overcomes the World

Fervent Faith: Discover How a Fervent Spirit is a Defense Against the Devil

Breakthrough!

Visit Jennifer online at:

www.jenniferleclaire.org

www.facebook.com/propheticbooks

www.twitter.com/propheticbooks

www.youtube.com/jnleclaire

www.flickr.com/propheticbooks

www.myspace.com/propheticbooks

www.connect.tangle.com/propheticbooks

CPSIA information can be obtained at www.ICGtesting.com
Printed in the USA
BVOW06s2210040915

416623BV00032B/1223/P

9 780981 979540